Praise for *Work Positive in a Negative World*

"*Work Positive in a Negative World* is about power, action and principle. It's helpful, breezy and most of all, paradigm shifting. In our always-on, negative oriented media culture, Dr. Joey's book is a gift. Read it and change your life for the better."

—TIM SANDERS, AUTHOR OF *TODAY WE ARE RICH*

"Read Dr. Joey's *Work Positive in a Negative World* and discover how to be one of those rare people that creates happiness wherever they go. If you do, you'll be labeled a big thinker and get to chart your own course."

—MICHAEL PORT, AUTHOR OF *BOOK YOURSELF SOLID*

"To apply the strategies in this book is to dramatically improve your business and life—period. Dr. Joey's insights into how to *Work Positive in a Negative World* provide a powerfully effective blueprint for achieving higher levels of success in all areas of your life, to the point where others will be specifically seeking you out because they want the chance to network with you!"

—IVAN MISNER, *NEW YORK TIMES* BESTSELLING AUTHOR AND FOUNDER OF BNI, THE WORLD'S LARGEST BUSINESS NETWORKING ORGANIZATION

"This book shows you how to unleash and channel your positive energy to get more done, better and faster than you ever thought possible."

—BRIAN TRACY, AUTHOR OF *HOW THE BEST LEADERS LEAD*

"When you get serious about becoming an Affluent Entrepreneur, you must read *Work Positive in a Negative World*. Dr. Joey is one of the best at coaching you to Perceive, Conceive, Believe, Achieve and Receive your Work Positive lifestyle!"

—PATRICK SNOW, INTERNATIONAL BESTSELLING AUTHOR OF *CREATING YOUR OWN DESTINY* AND *THE AFFLUENT ENTREPRENEUR*

"Dr. Joey Faucette has written a thought-provoking guide to the interior life. This is a book that strikes a deep chord of purpose."

—DR. RICHARD LEIDER, BESTSELLING AUTHOR OF *REPACKING YOUR BAGS* AND *THE POWER OF PURPOSE*

"Connecting with others is important, but connecting with positive others is supreme. Dr. Joey Faucette's *Work Positive in a Negative World* coaches you with great stories about how to 'Conceive' with other positive people and deal with negative people—'Eeyore Vampires'— without becoming one. Read this book today and watch your positive connections grow tomorrow!"

—Starr Hall, international speaker, fortune 1,000 marketing advisor, bestselling author of *Get Connected*

"If you want wisdom, truth and motivation to achieve your dreams, then listen to Dr. Joey. His words will help you soar!"

—Rochelle Riley, nationally syndicated columnist and author of *Raising a Parent*

"Every page of this book is an 'aha' experience and helps the reader find his or her own solutions to their daily challenges. You must buy, read and absorb this book and if you really desire success in life, buy some extra copies for your family, boss and work colleagues. You'll be doing yourself a huge favor!"

—Mike Podolinsky, CSP, Singapore Asia's Productivity Guru

"Dr. Joey's five core practices and the stories he tells in *Work Positive in a Negative World* make it easy to improve your attitude which determines your altitude and the impact you have on others."

—Hugh F. Gouldthorpe Jr., author of *I've Always Looked Up to Giraffes* and *How to Make a Giraffe Smile*

"*Work Positive in a Negative World* masterfully touches your inner core through stories that move you to do the next right thing, much like the classics *Think and Grow Rich* and *How to Win Friends and Influence People*."

—Bob Nicoll, Chief Paradigm Shifter, Remember the Ice, Alaska

"Dr. Joey has this rare and unique ability to tell stories and communicate wisdom that brings out the best in you. He truly coaches you to redefine your reality so you fulfill your dreams."

—Kirk Colford, insurance agent, Fort Lauderdale, Florida

"From time to time you encounter truly extraordinary people. These people have the unique gift of communication. I count Dr. Joey as one of these rare people."

—Marty Lambert, radio executive, Charlotte, North Carolina

Work Positive
in a Negative
World

Redefine Your Reality
and Achieve Your
Business Dreams

Dr. Joey Faucette

Entrepreneur
Press

Jere L. Calmes, Publisher
Cover Design: Andrew Welyczko
Production and Composition: Eliot House Productions

This publication is designed to provide accurate and authoritative information
in regard to the subject matter covered. It is sold with the understanding
that the publisher is not engaged in rendering legal, accounting or other
professional services. If legal advice or other expert assistance is required, the
services of a competent professional person should be sought.

Givers Gain® is a registered trademark, and has been reproduced with
permission, of BNI Enterprises, Inc.

Author Photo: Alice Abbott Photography

Library of Congress Cataloging-in-Publication Data
Faucette, Joey.
    Work positive: how to work positive in a negative world/by Joey
Faucette.
       p.   cm.
       Includes bibliographical references and index.
       ISBN-13: 978-1-59918-420-3
       ISBN-10: 1-59918-420-6
       1. Attitude (Psychology) 2. Success in business. I. Title.
    BF327.F38 2011
    650.1—dc22   2011008801

Printed in the United States of America

15 14 13 12 11   10 9 8 7 6 5 4 3 2 1

Let's Work Positive Linda!

Dr. Joe

To my wife, Rowan
who is the love of my life
and to
The One who loved us first.

Contents

SECTION ONE

"I PERCEIVE the POSITIVE at Work"

Contents

SECTION THREE

"I BELIEVE the POSITIVE at Work"

SECTION FOUR

"I ACHIEVE the POSITIVE at Work"

Contents

You Can Work Positive

> *"A dream you dream alone is only a dream.*
> *A dream you dream together is reality."*
>
> —John Lennon

How is it that we all do business in the same world, and yet do it so differently?

How is it that some of us perceive our current reality and interpret it as the worst of economic times, no opportunities, nothing will work out right, negative?

And others of us perceive our current reality and interpret it as the best of economic times, overflowing with opportunities, everything will work out fine, positive?

Linda started her own business, which became successful financially, but at a great cost. She rarely took a complete weekend off, and never took a vacation. Her husband and two young children went on trips without her.

After five years, she decided that now was the time to take a vacation and enjoy some extended time off, getting to know her husband again and enjoying her children. So she called her three vice presidents in for a meeting, and told them, "As you know, we've all worked hard to grow this company. I've ensured through these five years of hard work that each of you had some time away. But I didn't do for myself what I did for you.

"So the time has come for me to take an extended vacation. I'm taking the next year off to enjoy my family. The only way I can reasonably do this is to leave each of you in charge of running your departments.

"While I'm gone, I expect each of you to carry on as if I were here. And as an added bonus, I've deposited money in your department's account. Jill, you'll find $50,000 to invest in the business as you see fit. John, you're receiving $20,000 to invest in the business as you deem appropriate. And Paul, you'll find $10,000 to invest using your talents to grow this business. I'll be back a year from now and expect an accounting at that time." And Linda got up from her desk and left.

Jill, John, and Paul sat dumbfounded for a moment, and then stumbled over to the window overlooking the parking lot. "There she goes," Jill said. "She's really doing this."

"And for a whole year," John said. "Who would have thought it?"

Paul said, "Must be a trick or a test of some sort. She'd never leave us alone for that long with that much additional money."

Jill turned away from the window. "Well, you guys can stand here if you want to, but I've got $50,000 to invest in this business so I'm going to get busy." She walked out the door, down the hall, and toward her office.

"Yeah, me, too," said John, as he pulled his smartphone out to make a call, walking down the hall to his office.

"I still think it's a trick or something," Paul said, as he stood there in Linda's office.

A year passed more quickly than Linda imagined it would. She found herself back in her office, meeting with Jill, John, and Paul again. After chit-chatting about some of the highlights of her extended vacation, Linda said, "OK, Jill, tell me what you did with my $50,000 while I was gone."

Jill pulled a ledger sheet from her notebook and said, "Linda, I invested it in marketing a new division within our company to an underserved target group. You'll see at the bottom of this sheet that I doubled your $50,000. There's $100,000 profit there."

"Great work, Jill! That's exactly what I had hoped for. And because of your marvelous achievement, Jill, I'm making you a partner in the company. Here's a contract for you to read over and let me know what you think. Now John, it's your turn. What did you do with my $20,000 while I was on the beach relaxing?"

"You're gonna love this, Linda," John said as he pulled a ledger sheet from his notebook. "When you left, I studied our inventory liquidity and discovered that we've got some items that hang around a little too long in our warehouses, clogging up our cash flow. So I invested in new software and hardware for an updated inventory control system, negotiated with our vendors for tighter shipping, and well . . . you can see for yourself."

"Wow, John! You turned that department around to the tune of $40,000 by solving that problem. You are awesome, John. So let me do something awesome for you," and she handed him a contract. "Read this over and let me know what you think about becoming a partner in the company. Paul, it's your turn. Tell me something good!"

"Well, Linda," Paul said hesitantly, "I know you have very high standards, and I know you hate carelessness. You demand the best and don't tolerate a lot of mistakes. I was afraid I would disappoint you, so I wrote a check for the $10,000 you left me and put it in the company safe. And here it is, safe and sound—your $10,000."

Linda's face turned red, then scarlet. "Paul," she started slowly and methodically, "I've been gone a whole year, and the best thing you could do with $10,000 is to let it sit in the company safe?'

"Yes," Paul said. "It's all there."

"The least you could have done," Linda said while standing up, "was to have put it in a money market account somewhere. But you couldn't even do the least, could you, Paul? At least I would have gotten a little interest."

"I just thought it best to play it safe," Paul said.

"Play it safe?" Linda asked. Then she took a deep breath while thinking for a second. Then she said, "You know, Paul, you're right. Play it safe. Great policy. I'm going to play it safe, too."

She handed the $10,000 check to Jill and said, "Jill, here's $10,000. Invest it as you think best."

Then turning to Paul she said, "Paul, I'm going to play it safe some more. Go clean out your desk. You won't go out on a limb for me no matter how much fruit grows out there. So I can't go out on one for you, either. Take your things and leave. I can't afford to have you around any longer."

Who perceived the current reality and interpreted it as the worst of economic times, no opportunities, nothing will work out right, negative?

Who perceived the current reality and interpreted it as the best of economic times, overflowing with opportunities, everything will work out fine, positive?

Same situation. Same circumstances.

Paul redefined his reality and achieved nothing. He was fired.

Jill and John redefined their realities, met their goals, and fulfilled their dreams. They are partners in the company.

How is it that we all do business in the same world, and yet do it so differently?

I grew up hearing my grandparents talk about the Great Depression. If ever there was an example of our doing business in the same world and doing it so differently, it is the Great Depression. The economic woes are chronicled in volume after volume, and story after story my grandparents told me.

But did you know that Dale Carnegie wrote *How to Win Friends and Influence People* in the middle of the Great Depression? The book promised imminent success and sold more copies than any other book except the Bible up to that point. His other books continue to sell strongly and his training seminars are offered internationally today.

Did you know that during the Great Depression in Kentucky, a grandfather started pressure-cooking chicken with secret herbs and spices? People loved his chicken he served at his gas station so much that when the road moved and they stopped coming to his restaurant, despite going bankrupt, he took the chicken to them in his station wagon. His name was "Colonel" Harland Sanders, and you probably have eaten at a KFC (Kentucky Fried Chicken) somewhere along the way.

Did you know that two young electrical engineering graduates started an electrical machine business in a rented garage in Palo Alto, California, during the Great Depression? Bill Hewlett and Dave Packard officially became business partners in 1939. I enjoyed a flight from Phoenix to Denver recently with an employee of Hewlett Packard (HP) who was in charge of a conference with fellow employees from around the world. You probably have printed something out on one of their printers or used a computer with the "HP" label on it.

For most people, the Great Depression was the worst of times. For Dale Carnegie, Colonel Sanders, Hewlett and Packard, and a host of others, it was the best of times. Whom would you choose to do business like?

We can redefine reality and fulfill our dreams out of our core values, living our life priorities, and making our unique contributions to the world just like Dale Carnegie, Colonel Harland Sanders, Hewlett and Packard, and others who peered into the darkness around them and moved toward the pin dot of light.

How?

We redefine our reality and fulfill our dreams by learning to work positive. We discover how to do business positively in a negative world. The purpose of this book is to coach you to work positive, to redefine your reality in this negative world, and achieve your business dreams.

If a 9-year-old boy can learn to do it, so can you.

Like most 9-year-old boys, this one wanted a new bicycle. Three-speed bikes had just been released, and he wanted one in the worst sort of way. His parents told him he had a bike and to just be satisfied with it. He wasn't, and attempted to earn some summer spending money for the bike of his dreams the way most young boys do—mowing grass.

Only this little guy had allergies and asthma so extreme that his financial enterprise caused a viral infection in his lungs. Subsequently, he was hospitalized at the best pediatric allergy and asthma center in the world at that time, Duke University Hospital. One evening, the doctors told his mother, "We've done all we can."

His mother peered through the mist tent at the boy lying there in the hospital bed, looked deeply into his eyes, and said, "You can hold on through the night. I am positive that you can do this."

And he did. He recovered, came home, and, still determined to get a new bike, sold inscribed Christmas cards door-to-door in the heat of an August sun. His neighbors bought his cards; a lot of cards. He asked the folks with whom his dad worked, "How many beautiful Christmas cards with your family's name inscribed inside would you like?" They bought a lot of cards, too. He asked the folks at his church with the same result. Then people started calling him.

This 9-year-old boy who wanted a new three-speed bike sold so many inscribed Christmas cards that he bought his new bike . . . and a telescope . . . and a then-brand-new-technology cassette recorder/player.

Years later, the little boy grew up and was 17 years old when his dad came home early from a business trip one day and explained that an international company had bought the business for which he worked. They had pulled all of the cash out of it and were shutting it down, eliminating his job. "I don't know how we'll pay for your college," he said. The dad cried for the very first time in front of the son.

The now-teenaged boy remembered selling Christmas cards so well. He knew he could earn extra income to pay for college. So he drove to the local AM/FM radio station, and with absolutely no experience, walked into the owner's office and two hours later walked out with a job as a disc jockey. At first, he just worked weekends—the times no one else wanted to work. Within six months, he had the number-one rated afternoon drive show in the market.

He completed his bachelor's degree, paying for it as a Program Director at a radio station. Later he finished a master's degree and received a doctorate degree.

He went on to lead small, medium, and large organizations in turning around their operations. He liked to say, "I buy low and sell high." Each of these organizations achieved some type of historical record under his leadership.

Then one day, the 9-year-old boy reached midlife and decided it was time to start his own company, speaking to and coaching people to discover how they could redefine their reality and make their dreams come true, the same way Dale Carnegie, Colonel Sanders, Hewlett and Packard, and he had. So he started his very first business and called it, "Listen to Life."

I am that 9-year-old boy.

I studied work positive leaders—including my parents and grandparents—and have lived by their principles from a very early age. This book represents what I learned from them intellectually and what I discovered experientially in my own life.

One of the discoveries I made as I have coached over the years is that businesspeople often depend on the world to determine how much success they enjoy. Maybe you do, also. We allow our external circumstances to blueprint our internal conditions. We abdicate our birth right to achieve fulfillment through our businesses to the naysayers of negativity who chronically find something to complain about. Why do we do that? Perhaps we want someone to blame for our economic situation. Maybe we just don't want to be responsible for our lives generally and our businesses specifically.

Or, could it be we really want to enjoy the benefits of a positive personal and professional life, but don't know how and so do business overwhelmed by the weight of this negative world?

This world is negative, you know.

Do you doubt that for a second?

Then put this book down and turn on the TV to one of those 24/7 business news channels. Listen carefully to the news reporters' words. Notice the content of each story and its angle. It's unceasingly negative. Or, turn on your TV to a local station at 6:00 or 11:00 in the evening and watch your local news. If there is not enough bad news of personal devastation, disaster, and economic doom in your local community that day, they import stories from across the country of murders, fires, and business closings fed down the affiliate lines.

Or, pick up your newspaper and just read the lead headline for a week. Track the content and how it is reported. Something is always rotten in Denmark. It's Enron every day. It's only news if the man bites the dog, not if the dog bites the man, and there's a whole lot of biting going on, isn't there? If there's not, there ought to be, so let's publish an editorial predicting the end of the economy as we know it.

Or, listen to talk radio in the afternoon for a week. Sure, try out different personalities on different stations. You will discover a great deal of commonality, if not in viewpoint, certainly in style— attack and destroy the other side, and promote your own. Political and business Chicken Littles report "the sky is falling," and it is someone else's fault. "If the world would just do what I say, I could solve all the problems because I am the hero" fills the airwaves all afternoon. We drown daily in a tsunami of negative egocentricity from our public airwaves.

Let's get more personal. Ask someone you know who is usually negative, whose life is unfulfilling, whose business dreams have died, "How are you?" Then listen to the litany of problems, predicaments, and pathos.

You didn't have to turn on the TV or radio, pick up a newspaper, or phone a friend to see if I'm right, did you? You know the answer. The world is negative.

And you're trying to do business in it.

So how's that working for you?

But maybe you're wondering, "Is the world really all that negative? Or, is it just reported as such?"

If you participate in the world's negativity and allow the world to define your reality, then it simply does not matter. You choose to define your business world as negative. However, if you redefine your reality—that is, you choose to work positive in a negative world—you will fulfill your business dreams and enjoy the benefits of your positive life with your family and friends.

That's why this book is so important right now.

Sure, there are a ton of problems to tackle immediately in the world from spiraling economic crises to natural disasters to nuclear proliferation to human suffering from genocide wars. We absolutely, positively must resolve each of them.

However, if we continue to bring the same mental models to these problems, we will get more of what we already have. The purpose of this book is to coach you to start being positive in the professional and personal dimensions of who you are in this negative world and sustain it. As you do, you perceive new solutions to old business challenges. You conceive business with other positive people and discover ways of delivering these new solutions. You believe that your business reality can be redefined and dreams fulfilled, that these old problems are entrepreneurial opportunities in disguise. Then you achieve the impossible. You redefine your reality and fulfill your dreams, and the world around you takes on new meaning pregnant with fresh core values and satisfaction gained from business successes. New economic resolutions appear all around you as you make your unique contributions to the world. In that moment of achievement, you realize that you have more than anything else received the benefits of the work positive lifestyle. So you say, "Thank you!" You give away all the positivity you can as you lead your company by serving others. And amazingly, the cycle of working positive turns again and you find yourself receiving even more in your business. So you start another business, putting more people to work, who catch your positive contagion. And another business starts . . . and another . . . just like with Jill and John, Dale Carnegie, Colonel Sanders, and Hewlett and Packard . . . and me.

That's the kind of life you really want!

You can have this kind of life. This book is more than 50 years in its making. At least, that's my experience with it, but the great truths written on these pages are eternal. They precede me by at least a couple of millennia, perhaps more. I simply have received them. It is my pleasure and obligation to share them with you.

Meditate on these great truths as you redefine your reality and fulfill your business dreams in a work positive lifestyle. As you do, you'll discover reading pit stops along the way. That is me flagging you over to "Ponder Your Work Positive Life for a Moment . . ." Idle in the pits for a few minutes or a few hours, depending on which lap you are on, how successfully you achieved positivity, or how much negativity is smeared on your windshield. Consider your business life while you refuel.

As you refuel, share what you're pondering. Let's have a conversation about what's working well and what you hope to improve. On Twitter, use the hashtag #wpnw to mark your comments. I'll look for you and we'll extend our conversation beyond this book. Let's form a community of entrepreneurs, business owners, and executives who Work Positive.

Also, at the end of each chapter, you'll find a "Grab and Go" summary. These quick statements crystallize the major points and also give you a mile marker to return to when you want a quick, refreshing drink of positive energy. Doing business every day dehydrates you. These pages give you a pick-me-up.

Some of our fellow business travelers enjoy reading this book together and then talking about what they discover along the journey. As you will find, that's complementary conceiving at its best that strengthens your believing, and achieving, and receiving your work positive lifestyle. Others first read this book introspectively, pondering deep within themselves how to work positive in a negative world and fulfill their business dreams. Later they talk about it with others.

However you approach this book, the ultimate reality is that you actually can enjoy a work positive lifestyle while doing business in this negative world. This book is about how. Thanks for the privilege of sharing the journey with you.

"I PERCEIVE the POSITIVE at Work"

"I Perceive"

"I am an old man and have known a great many
troubles, but most of them never happened."
—Mark Twain

I was lying flat on my back in the grassy outfield, trying to come
around. I had drifted back from my third-base position for the
Little League team White Sox into shallow left field to catch a fly
ball. I had missed the ball with my glove and instead caught it with
my forehead.

I remember hearing, "Son, you've got to keep your eye on the
ball."

Little comfort when your head is killing you and your ego is
dead with embarrassment.

Around that time, I walked into my fourth-grade classroom, sat
down at my desk, and pulled out my notebook paper and pencil
just as Mrs. Wheeler ordered. It was time for math, and having
announced that, she flipped on the overhead projector. More math
problems, but for some reason, I couldn't make them out. Assuming

that this then-new technology wasn't functioning correctly, I asked Mrs. Wheeler, "Would you please focus the problems on the screen? I can't see them."

"Well, you're sitting right under them. I don't know why you can't," she said. "Stop trying to get attention and just do your work, Joey."

Yet another blow to my already crucified ego.

Now fast-forward 30-something years. I'm sitting in my favorite recliner, trying to read a book and not doing so well.

"There's not enough light in this room," I told my wife. "And have you noticed how small they're making the print these days? Must be a cost-cutting move to save paper."

I played yo-yo with the book trying to get it the right distance for me to read, discovered I couldn't, and said, "My arms must have shrunk from all those hot showers during my teenaged years."

The last vestiges of my ego snuck away in middle age.

I caught two more fly balls with my forehead before they figured it out. I can still remember the first fly ball I squeezed into my glove, breathing a sigh of relief after they figured it out.

I saw my grades go from A's to C's before they figured it out. I can still feel that sense of justified explanation when I walked into Mrs. Wheeler's classroom after they figured it out.

I noticed that I was reading a lot less before I figured it out. I can recall today that sense of magical wonder when I could read again with no difficulty.

What did we figure out? My perception was off. I needed glasses in fourth grade. Later, I needed bifocals.

What about your mental perception of how your business is going? How do you know when that is blurry?

Discovering how you perceive your company is the first step to enjoying a work positive lifestyle in a negative world. Sometimes it can take a while to figure it out, can't it? Sometimes we don't want to figure it out.

Living in a negative world, our first reaction is to blame our economic problems on this negative world, much like I experienced with my vision.

"Son, keep your eye on the ball."

"Stop trying to get attention and just do your work, Joey."

"There's not enough light in this room."

It's so easy to just stop right there and not figure it out; blame an economic downturn on the negative world, and settle for less than our businesses can be.

Instead, let's figure it out.

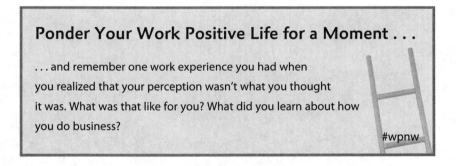

Ponder Your Work Positive Life for a Moment . . .

. . . and remember one work experience you had when you realized that your perception wasn't what you thought it was. What was that like for you? What did you learn about how you do business?

#wpnw

Knowing how to perceive the positive in this negative world is the first step to actually enjoying the benefits of a work positive lifestyle expressed through your company. Perception is the mental dynamic of a positive life in your business. You choose the thoughts you focus on as they relate to your business, be they positive or negative. Let's look at how we perceive our businesses, the obstacles to perceiving them positively, and then how we can perceive a positive business life and be successful.

CHAPTER 2

Focus Your Thoughts

"I'm not sure what the future holds, but I do know that I'm going to be positive and not wake up feeling desperate. As my dad said, 'Nic, it is what it is, it's not what it should have been, not what it could have been, it is what it is.'"

—Nicole Kidman

I'm sure you've played the game where someone mentions an object—a dancing bear wearing a red vest with a black top hat—and tells you not to think about it. Of course, what's the first thing that flashes in your mind? That dreaded dancing bear wearing a red vest in a black top hat. Your mind focuses your thoughts very quickly and with just a little suggestion.

So why is it such a challenge for most of us to focus our thoughts about our businesses on our chosen, positive subjects? Because your mind focuses your thoughts very quickly and with just a little suggestion. Unless you discipline your mind, that is coach it to filter out some thoughts and focus on others, it will hone in on whatever attention grabber presents itself. Your mind is like a muscle. You exercise it to strengthen it to do what you want it to do.

Mental Surgery Is Necessary

This truth became real to me some years ago when my family and I bought a small farm. My wife's lifelong dream was to live on such a farm and own a horse boarding business. Of course our two daughters loved the idea as well . . . until it came time to plant the fence posts around the pastures. My two employees called in sick.

So I phoned a friend or two who helped me plant fence posts. It was back-breaking labor, but it wasn't my back that I injured. It was my shoulder. The repetitive motions created scar tissue in my left shoulder joint that made my shoulder "freeze up"—literally, the doctor called it "frozen shoulder."

As a part of the physical therapy following surgery, the doctor and the therapist explained to me that the shoulder joint operates out of what is actually a system of supporting muscles in my upper chest and back. When these muscles weaken, the joint is left to pull more of its weight than intended. My weak muscles left my shoulder joint vulnerable, which is why the scar tissue built up and the shoulder froze.

While I'm completely healed from the surgery and no longer go to physical therapy, I make sure that I am in a fitness center as a regular part of my schedule, focusing on those machines that build up the muscle groups around my shoulder. I can literally feel the weakness in that joint when I don't take time to exercise. The shoulder works in tip-top shape when I maintain a consistent exercise schedule. By focusing on strengthening my shoulder, I stay out of the operating room and enjoy a pain-free life.

Just as my shoulder has a muscle group that requires strengthening, so does your mind. The other four steps in this process of work positive—conceive, believe, achieve, and receive—comprise that muscle group. A flabby, unfit mind simply chases whatever thought about your business enters it—or, whatever thought someone else suggests about it, positive or negative. Your mind freezes up; that is, mental scar tissue builds up in your mind, and you become susceptible to whatever thought shows up. Mental surgery then becomes necessary to remove the scar tissue of those negative thoughts that moved you to behave in your business in an unhealthy manner.

Here's how your mind works. You watch a report on a business channel that says the economy is contracting, that manufacturing is down, that consumer confidence is at its lowest point, and "top economists" (whoever they are) predict a drastic drop in spending in the next quarter. Now, your business has grown stronger for the last six consecutive quarters. Your bottom line is firm. But what do you do when your best vendor calls to confirm your next quarter's order? You shrink the order despite your track record of success.

Think not? OK, let's bring it home. You're watching your favorite TV program, and a commercial comes on for a snack food. You weren't hungry before, but suddenly you are. The next thing you know, you're getting up and heading to the kitchen for snack food.

The power of suggestion is so strong. Your mind received the impression, activated a hunger impulse, and triggered your legs to move. You really didn't even think about it. It just happened.

But what if you focus your thoughts? In this instance, what if you have made a conscious decision to cut out snacks between meals because you realize that your metabolism has slowed significantly at middle age? Your mind is made up—your priority of losing weight takes precedence over the commercial's suggestion. You think about getting a snack, but decide against it because it is more important to be healthy than to chase a snack commercial into the kitchen. Your mind was made up before the commercial ever appeared.

But maybe you're thinking, "It's not that easy to focus my thoughts, especially when it comes to my company."

Actually it is. Your mind was made to focus. In fact, it focuses on something every minute of your life, even when you're sleeping.

Still not sure?

OK, as soon as you read the opening paragraph about the dancing bear in the red vest and black top hat, what did you see in your mind? The same dancing bear in the red vest and black top hat that you see now, right?

Your mind focuses on something every minute of every day and night of your life. It is the way your brain functions. The question is not if you focus your mind, but on what?

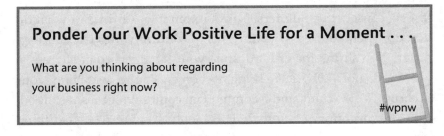

Ponder Your Work Positive Life for a Moment . . .

What are you thinking about regarding
your business right now?

#wpnw

You See What You Look For

Let's say you are interested in buying a new vehicle. You go to the dealer's car lot and look at a white Honda Accord. You even decide to test-drive it. Wow, it sure is a nice driving vehicle. You really like it. You can see yourself in it, but the salesperson just won't get the price right for you. You leave the lot to think about the purchase some more.

As you turn out of the dealer's lot and drive down the street, guess what you see? A white Honda Accord. You think, "That's interesting."

You pull out onto the expressway and merge into traffic right behind . . . a white Honda Accord.

You look across the median at the traffic headed in the opposite direction. What kind of car passes you? That's right, a white Honda Accord.

You think to yourself, "There are white Honda Accords everywhere!"

Now are there really? Of course not. In fact, there are no more white Honda Accords on the road that day than there were on any previous day. Your mind simply was focused on the white Honda Accord you just drove.

You saw what you chose to see.

You focus your mind every minute of every day and night on something. It's just a matter of your mental choices.

What do you choose to perceive when it comes to your business?

Where is your work focus—on the positive or the negative?

There is no denying that the world contains negative mental energy for you to perceive. You can't achieve a work positive lifestyle in business simply by denying the existence of negativity in the world. The world is negative around you. It is illegitimate to expect any business environment simply to overwhelm you with positivity. Your customers or clients, your banker, your attorney, your CPA, your Chamber of Commerce, your _____ (insert the rest of them here) are not filling your calendar with appointments, nor standing in line to fill your mind with positive affirmations about your business. You focus your mind, which is going to focus on something anyway, on the positive dimensions of your business into which you want to live despite the negative world. The work positive lifestyle you want will be yours because you choose it. The positive business you grow is yours by choice.

Think about your choice to perceive this way. Vultures fly over the desert, looking for dead animals. They search for fallen carcasses.

Hummingbirds fly over the same desert, looking for something different. Hummingbirds look for flowers growing from a cactus or near a pond. They search for floral displays.

The difference between the vulture and the hummingbird is what they're looking for. They fly over the same desert. One looks for death. The other looks for life.

As it is with the vulture and hummingbird, so it is with you and me. As we fly over the business landscape that surrounds us, we're looking for something. We choose what we're looking for—death or life, failures or successes, losses or leverage; the negative or the positive.

Then we live our choices. Those choices determine how positively successful we are. Those choices establish whether we keep the doors open and lights turned on in our businesses or the bank locks it up and it goes dark.

We see what we look for.

My wife and I were eating together in a restaurant when the owner approached us. We're friends in addition to being patrons so I stood and hugged her. She put her hands around my waist, and said, "I saw you walking across the parking lot. Have you lost weight?" as she patted my sides.

"No," I said, "must be this floppy shirt."

"Well, I definitely think you've lost weight," she said.

I stood back for a moment and noticed her waistline. She had lost weight, and noticeably so.

"You're the one who's lost weight," I said.

"Well, yes, I have," she replied.

A few minutes later as my wife and I continued our meal, some friends came over to say hello. Again, I stood and hugged. This woman also hugged my waist, patted my sides, and said, "Have you gained weight?"

"No," I replied, "must be this floppy shirt."

"Well," she said, "I definitely think you've gained some weight."

I stood back for a moment and noticed that she had gained some weight and noticeably so. Fortunately, I had the good sense not to comment on it.

I sat back down, and my wife started laughing. I joined her and said, "So which is it? Have I lost or gained weight?"

"I wouldn't wear that floppy shirt anymore if I were you," she said.

So what did we learn more about in these two conversations—my state of weight or the two women's?

We see what we look for. How do you perceive your business?

Show Me What You Can Do

When our daughters were much younger, I chose to spend as much time as I could with them. As little girls, they wanted to be with me and we enjoyed a lot of fun experiences together.

For me, life (and business, too) is an opportunity for adventure so we were constantly doing things like hiking up a mountain or fishing in a pond or fixing something around our home. Invariably, they would say, "Daddy, I can't do it."

My response was always the same: "Don't tell me what you can't do. Show me what you can."

As they grew older and life became more complicated, they said, "Daddy, I can't do it." And I replied, "Don't tell me what you can't do. Show me what you can."

In fact, I'm sure that at my funeral, one of them will talk about one of Daddy's favorite sayings was, "Don't tell me what you can't do. Show me what you can."

Why is that one of my favorite sayings? Think about it. It is so easy for us to fill our minds with what we can't do. That's a never-ending list for me.

Right now, in fact, I could say to myself, "There's always something I can't do. In fact, now that I think about it, there's no reason in the world I should ever think that anyone anywhere on this planet would want to read this book. I don't know why I wrote it! I wasted all this time, energy, and money on a book that was supposed to bring me speaking engagements and coaching opportunities so I can transform business people's negative lives into work positive lifestyles."

See what I mean? Of course it's not just you and me who choose to focus on that "can't do" list. We all do at times. Since your mind focuses on something, anything, it will go to that never-ending list, especially in times of frustration or perceived failure.

It is so much more empowering to focus your mind on what you can do. No, you might not be able to do correctly what you're attempting on the first try. However, finding something you can do related to the task, doing it, and focusing on that accomplishment creates a positive perception in your mind. That positive perception then becomes the jet fuel that releases your imagination to work on the rest of the task that presents such a challenge. With that high-octane fuel, your imagination soars to new heights of accomplishment in your business. You exercise the positive muscle group of your mind, focus on profit-enriching activities, and pretty soon that which seemed impossible about your business becomes not only doable, but you say to yourself, "I can see my business this way all the time!"

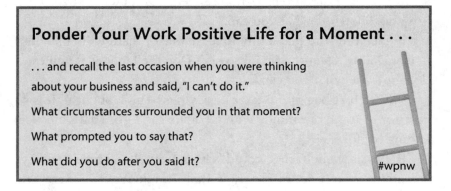

Ponder Your Work Positive Life for a Moment . . .

. . . and recall the last occasion when you were thinking about your business and said, "I can't do it."

What circumstances surrounded you in that moment?

What prompted you to say that?

What did you do after you said it?

#wpnw

The Perception You Change May Be Your Own

One day, my associate and I were working on a task together. She was in her office, crunching numbers or something else I'm not as gifted at as she is, and I was in my office. She called to me from her office and said, "Look out your window and tell me what you see."

So I turned away from my desk, stared out the window, and said, "All I see is a house that needs to be torn down." Literally it was falling in on itself.

"No, look again," she said.

I replied, "I don't need to. Seriously, it's beyond repair."

She walked into my office, raised the blinds, pointed and said, "Not the house. What else do you see?"

Almost as if for the very first time, I saw them—beautiful, lilac-colored, in full bloom, azaleas that stood several feet high in front of the house.

"Aren't they beautiful?" she said.

And I said, "Yes, if you choose to see them."

It is extremely easy for our minds to focus on the negative in our companies, like vultures trolling for death or city inspectors looking for run-down houses. Instead, we can choose to focus our mental energy on perceiving the positive in our businesses, like hummingbirds sniffing out flowers. It's a choice we make, consciously or unconsciously. Our minds focus on something related to doing business all the time. It's just a matter of how we guide our thoughts to perceive the positive, choosing the best qualities about how we do business, not the worst; things to praise our employees about, not things to curse them for; the beautiful way in which our customers buy our products and use our services, not the ugly few who demand a refund.

Our younger daughter helped me learn how to choose the positive to perceive when she was about 4 years old. I really enjoy feeding the birds on our farm in winter. I set up a bird feeder in our backyard almost every winter. The problem is that squirrels love bird feeders, or more specifically, bird seed.

So I waged war on the bird-seed-stealing squirrels one winter. I borrowed an air rifle, and started looking for the "mangy tree rats." I looked for the squirrels every time I walked by our bay window, just waiting for them to show themselves so that I could grab the rifle, sneak outside around the corner of our home, and shoot them. I even put our younger daughter on alert—"Honey, let me know if you see a squirrel on our bird feeder."

That is, until one day she looked up at me and said, "Daddy, we used to look out the window for pretty birds. Now we look for ugly squirrels."

When she said that, I realized that all the joy of my bird feeder was gone. I wasn't looking for pretty birds and their magnificent colors anymore, but ugly, drab squirrels that I could shoot.

It's easy to see only the ugly, drab squirrels that invade your company, isn't it? Those bushy-tailed thieves would steal our positive lives at work . . . if we let them. It's easy to stop looking for the beautiful qualities about our businesses, to cease listening for the lovely songs, whether they be the cha-ching of the cash register or the relieved look on a customer's face when you solve a problem with them, to miss the brilliant colors of the relationships you enjoy with employees and clients alike . . . if we so choose.

I put down my weapon. I stopped looking for the ugly. I looked for the beautiful in life . . . again. And I found it . . . because I looked for it.

You see what you choose to see.

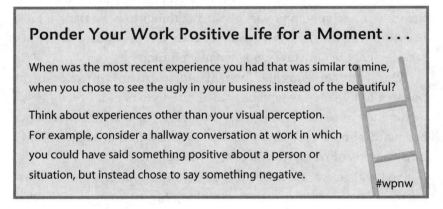

Ponder Your Work Positive Life for a Moment . . .

When was the most recent experience you had that was similar to mine, when you chose to see the ugly in your business instead of the beautiful?

Think about experiences other than your visual perception. For example, consider a hallway conversation at work in which you could have said something positive about a person or situation, but instead chose to say something negative.

#wpnw

Your Mind Constantly Perceives

I sat, relaxing with a newspaper, enjoying some quiet time early one morning before the demands of my day started. All of a sudden, a bird began making all kinds of noises just outside the window. At first I ignored it, but it kept on. So finally, I got up to investigate.

And as I stepped out on the porch, I saw the bird—a baby mockingbird—perched in a Japanese maple, squawking at Maybelle, our cat, who sat on the porch, staring off across the horse pasture. The bird who bothered me didn't seem to bother Maybelle at all.

Maybelle saw me on the porch and sauntered over, rubbing herself against my legs, letting me know that I had permission to pet her, which I did for a couple of minutes while she purred. All the while, this baby bird was still screaming at us, but Maybelle just didn't mind. She focused on the beauty of that quiet morning, letting me pet her—anything but the noisy bird. She knew the bird was there, but chose to ignore it.

There is always someone or something squawking at you about your business, making it challenging for you to perceive a work positive lifestyle, isn't there? Sometimes it seems like there are more squawkers than normal, doesn't it? You go to work and there's a squawking employee complaining about the cheap coffee you provide. Or, there's a squawking employer who thinks you're a Superperson and can leap tall problems in a single bound. Or, there's a squawking customer who's convinced you overcharged her a nickel.

As if work didn't provide you with enough squawking, you go home and the laundry has yet to put itself in the washing machine and the vacuum cleaner is still in the closet and the pot roast has not hopped into the crock pot and it's supper time and like hungry little birds, your kids are squawking, "We're hungry. What's for supper?"

It's challenging to focus on the positive at such times, isn't it?

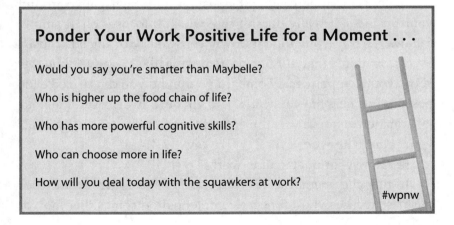

Ponder Your Work Positive Life for a Moment . . .

Would you say you're smarter than Maybelle?

Who is higher up the food chain of life?

Who has more powerful cognitive skills?

Who can choose more in life?

How will you deal today with the squawkers at work?

#wpnw

Imagination—Your Mental Jet Fuel

We can learn much from Maybelle about how to perceive the positive life at work and focus our thoughts. Maybelle chose to ignore the baby mockingbird, but she did more than that. Initially, she chose to ignore the bird and look out across the pastures, basking in the warm sunlight. She didn't just turn away from something negative—the bird; she turned into something positive—the sun's warmth and later my petting.

To grow a work positive lifestyle, you have to do more than turn your mind away or ignore the worst, the things to curse, the ugly squawkers. To enjoy a positive life at work, you choose to perceive the positive around you, focusing your mind on the best practices you can put into place in your business, the things about your business that are worthy of praising because they're working well, and the beautiful relationships you have with employees, vendors, suppliers, and customers.

If you simply choose to ignore the negative aspects of your business, you create a mental vacuum. Your mind abhors a mental vacuum. Remember—your mind constantly focuses, whether you're awake or asleep. Your mind searches and discovers a thought or thing to fill itself with regardless of your intentions.

The jet fuel that powers your mental focus—your imagination— is equally good at perceiving the positive and the negative around your business. It really doesn't care which it focuses on. It simply follows the trail you guide it down, consciously or unconsciously. So if you think that simply by removing the negative thoughts about your company that bombard your mind you can perceive the positive business life you want, you will quickly discover that your imagination abhors a vacuum and will work to fill it. Usually it fills your mind with worry.

See how your imagination works?

It fills the mental void with worry. Worrying about your business focuses you on negative potential outcomes that may or may not become reality. Your mind requires filling with something, anything, even if that something only exists in your imaginary business.

Ponder Your Work Positive Life for a Moment . . .

What were you worried about in your business last year?

Can you remember?

#wpnw

PerceiveThrough the Fog

Let's say that you understand how your imagination works and choose to focus on the positive, ignoring the negative aspects of your business. But your imagination starts asking for more information and you don't have it. You allow your thoughts to follow the rabbit of your imagination down that hole.

"What if the bank calls my note due early because I had a down quarter?"

"What if my key employee quits to start his own business?"

"What if my spouse says I'm never home and leaves me for someone else because I cut payroll and am having to do the jobs of three people now?"

What happens when you descend into this imaginary hole? It's almost like a mental fog rolls in and because you cannot see into the future far enough to satisfy the insatiable appetite of your imagination, worry slips in on cat's paws.

Or, horse's hooves.

The kitchen in our home has a bay window that lets us look down the hill and across the horse pastures. It's really quite a beautiful sight . . . except when the fog rolls in. When the fog rolls in, you can't see down the hill and across the pastures. That means that you can't see the horses and make sure that they're OK. That's when our imaginations start asking for more information than we can supply and it's easy for us to worry.

Our minds immediately go through about 5,392 bad things that could happen to the horses, each one worse than another: a snake could bite one on the nose, one could step in a hole and hurt itself, one could get sick and die because we didn't call the vet in time, and the list goes on and on. Of course, so far, none of these things have ever happened to us, with or without the fog. But since we can't see, we worry.

I suspect you're that way, also—what you can't see, like the "What if . . ." future of your company, you worry about. And I'll bet so far in your life few if any of the things you worry about actually happened. And yet, that does not keep you from worrying, does it? You allow your imagination to take control of your perception and negative thoughts crop up.

It happens to all of us.

The question is: What do we do about it?

Mow Your Negative Mental Broom Straw

One thing you can do is to mow your negative mental broom straw.

I got on my tractor on a beautiful winter day and mowed a portion of our pasture. Now you may be thinking, "Dr. Joey, nothing grows in a pasture over the winter."

Well, not exactly. Broom straw grows over the winter. Occasionally the soil nutrients are a little off of what's best for growing grass and broom straw jumps up over the winter. It competes with the spring grass for nutrients, water, and sunlight. Horses eat grass and pick around the broom straw. So I mow the broom straw.

When your imagination takes control of your perception, negative thinking crops up like broom straw. It competes for nutrients in your mind. Have you ever noticed that one negative thought breeds another? And another? And pretty soon, there's an entire field of negative mental broom straw growing in your mind?

You can choose to mow down your negative thoughts and in their place plant positive thoughts. Let me share with you a couple of ways to do that.

First, start each day by opening your mind to positive dynamics of your work positive lifestyle.

Each morning, I get up early to read and meditate. My favorite place to spend this quiet time planting positive perceptions in my mind is in our kitchen, rocking in the chair where I cradled our infant daughters. There are windows beside the bay window and on a cool morning, I'll raise them.

One morning, I sat sipping my coffee, rocking and meditating on the day ahead, eyes closed. I realized that the window was shut so I got up and raised it.

As I raised it, a bird was singing the most beautiful song, welcoming the day and gifting the world with his music. I enjoyed the bird song as a kind of morning serenade. Then I thought, "I'm sure this bird was singing before I opened the window, but I either didn't hear it or didn't pay attention to it."

Doing business today is a lot like that. There is so much positivity to perceive, but if the window to your mind isn't open and you aren't still and listening, you miss the music.

I find that by making sure I invest time every morning to throw open the window to my mind, I focus my mind on and grow positive thoughts. I start each day choosing to think positively about my businesses. I literally visualize positive activities. My mind focuses on something anyway. I may as well guide its focus to positive achievements, right?

I avoid all "push media" such as TV and radio in the mornings. Why allow them to define my reality negatively by pushing on me their revision of it? I stay informed by "pull media" such as internet news sites where I scan headlines and pull the stories I choose to read and watch. This positive, proactive approach guarantees

I focus as I choose rather than abdicating my choice to network executives. The direct, positive impact on my business is, I avoid becoming what Jim Rohn called a "financial pygmy" and grow mentally more positive, which propels me to success.

Second, I end each day by choosing to think positively about my businesses and my life in general. Every night, I get in bed a little while before I want to go to sleep. I relax, close my eyes, and name three things I'm thankful for that happened that day. I plant in my mind an attitude of gratitude that cultivates in my sleep overnight.

I am as specific as possible. Instead of saying, "I'm thankful for my wife," I say, "I'm thankful for my wife and her generous gift of her time in running three errands for me today." Or, instead of just saying, "I'm grateful for all new friends who bought my books today," I say, "I'm grateful for my friend Louise, who after our coaching session today bought copies of my book for her entire staff, contracted with me to do group coaching with them, and signed up for our online video coaching for her executive team meetings."

Being specific seems to help. I feel more refreshed than usual the next morning because I've put these positive perceptions of gratitude into my mind and my brain processed them overnight. Remember: Your mind is knit together in such a way that your thoughts focus on your chosen subject day and night.

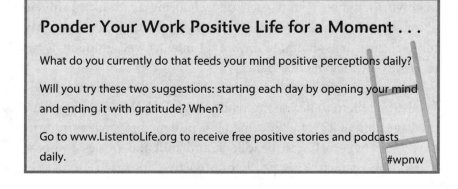

Ponder Your Work Positive Life for a Moment . . .

What do you currently do that feeds your mind positive perceptions daily?

Will you try these two suggestions: starting each day by opening your mind and ending it with gratitude? When?

Go to www.ListentoLife.org to receive free positive stories and podcasts daily.

#wpnw

Focus on the Good Soil

One of the things I enjoy doing around our farm is planting grass seed in the horse pastures. One fall, I bought some sacks of good seed and loaded them in the spreader on the back of my tractor. I scattered the seed everywhere I could.

I noticed in the days following that the horses had beat down a path through the pasture. They walk that same path every day so it's a hardened path where no grass grows. Since the ground was hard, the birds came and ate the grass seed off of the path.

Some of the seed I scattered wound up in a pile of rocks I collected from the pasture and stacked up around the base of an oak tree. It grew pretty quickly and I could see the new green sprouts, but that's about as big as it ever grew. The roots were shallow and the hot spring sun scorched it.

Some of the seed I scattered went outside of the fence line and over into a really thick area where blackberry thorn bushes grow. From what I could perceive, the grass took root and shot up for a little while, but evidently it just couldn't compete for sunlight and nutrients with the taller, more mature blackberry bushes. So it died.

The rest of the seed I scattered fell on parts of the pasture that were good soil. They grew up in the spring, took solid root, and just kept growing. In fact, it wasn't too long before I could turn the horses back into that pasture and they just loved all that new grass. The grass produced far more than I ever imagined.

After reading this chapter, you may have any of several reactions.

You could say, "I just don't get it, all this talk about how my mind constantly focuses on something all the time." You have been living the negative life so long that you are the path my horses beat down—hard—so the good seed of this chapter can't penetrate your mind.

You might say, "Yeah, I love it!" and start practicing focusing your thoughts about your business so you can enjoy a work positive lifestyle, achieve a little success, and say, "I got it" and put this book down. Your experience will be like the grass that grew in the rock pile. When the heat of an economic downturn overwhelms you—and it will—you will wilt and give up.

You may say, "I'm going to turn my thoughts away from the negative," but not choose to fill your mind with positive perceptions. Worry rolls into your imagination like fog. The weeds of worry choke your imagination and keep you from positively growing your business.

Or, perhaps you read this chapter and said to yourself, "This is really good stuff. I'm focusing my thoughts on the positive aspects of my business, but I want more." You, my friend, are ready for a beautiful growing experience that will feed you for the rest of your life. Keep reading . . .

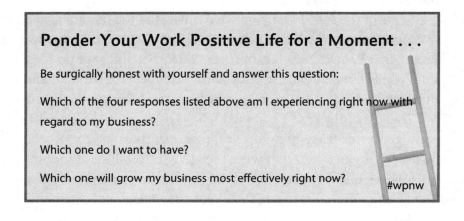

Ponder Your Work Positive Life for a Moment . . .

Be surgically honest with yourself and answer this question:

Which of the four responses listed above am I experiencing right now with regard to my business?

Which one do I want to have?

Which one will grow my business most effectively right now?

#wpnw

Grab & Go

As you "Focus Your Thoughts," remember:

1. As you learn to grow your business positively, the perception you change may be your own.

2. You see what you're looking for in your business:

   a. A white Honda Accord

   b. Carcasses or cacti

   c. A dilapidated house or stunning azaleas

   d. Ugly squirrels or beautiful birds

   e. Squawking birds or a growing business

   f. Lost or gained weight

   g. "Don't tell me what you can't do. Show me what you can."

3. Worry fogs your perception about your business.

4. Mow the mental broom straw out of your perceptions about your business.

5. Raise the window of your work positive lifestyle as your business sings to you.

6. Focus your thoughts on being the positive-soil leader of your company.

7. The seed of your business is good. Enrich the soil.

CHAPTER 3

Avoid Only Familiar Thoughts

"As a single footstep will not make a path on the earth, so a single thought will not make a pathway in the mind. To make a deep physical path, we walk again and again. To make a deep mental path, we must think over and over the kind of thoughts we wish to dominate our lives."

—Henry David Thoreau

S everal generations ago, a country doctor, who was an avid fox hunter, often took his dogs along and turned them loose to chase foxes while he waited for women to deliver their babies. There was also a barber in the area whose shop was a favorite loafing place for telling stories. The barber listened to the doctor tell his stories, had never been fox hunting, and so persuaded the doctor to take him.

The two went up a mountain highway and turned the dogs loose. Soon the chase began at a furious pace. The gentlemen sat in the front seat of the truck, and occasionally the doctor would nudge the barber and say, "Just listen to that music." The barber listened carefully and said nothing.

This same routine happened every few minutes until finally the barber said, "Doc, I've listened closely for several minutes now, and I can't hear the music because your dogs keep barking."

One man's music is another man's dogs barking.

Sometimes the familiar gets in the way of the work positive lifestyle we chase.

Super-Efficient or Basically Lazy?

When considering how you perceive your business positively you must think about how your brain functions. Like the doctor and the barber chose two different ways to hear the dogs, you can see your brain as super-efficient or basically lazy. Either way, here's what happens as you perceive your business:

1. A perception of your company enters your mind through some sense.
2. Your brain begins to sort the information.
3. Part of the sorting process is searching the catalog in which information has been stored previously. Your mind wants to place this new information in a folder labeled "Familiar." In other words, if it resembles something you've stored before, your brain wants to lump it in that category.
4. If it does not fit in a current category and your brain has no idea where to file it, it tries to throw it out, or at least put it in the "Recycle Bin" in hopes that you empty and delete it later.
5. It is at this moment that you say something like, "I don't understand" or "I've never done it this way before" or "You've got to be kidding me!" or "I can't hear the music because your dogs keep barking." You label the unfamiliar perception as "Negative," and toss it.

The neural pathways in your brain are like interstate highways. Familiar thoughts course up and down them like BMWs and Mercedes-Benzes on the German Autobahn. Unfamiliar thoughts are like Vespas and mopeds trying to run the Autobahn. Either move over or get off the interstate. That's the way your mind treats them, especially the first time you encounter such a thought.

The world is constantly changing, and so is your business's context. How do you deal with so much change?

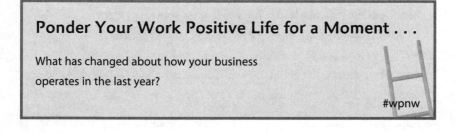

Ponder Your Work Positive Life for a Moment . . .

What has changed about how your business
operates in the last year?

#wpnw

Repeat After Me: "Repetition, Repetition, Repetition . . ."

Do you remember when your third-grade teacher showed you all those multiplication tables and said you had to memorize them? What was your reaction? "No way," right?

Today you know them. You carved out some new neural pathways in your brain. You created a new folder named "Times Tables."

How did you do it?

Repetition.

Your parent or grandparent made you sit down and stare at them, saying them over and over to yourself, speaking them out loud to someone, until you got every single one of them correct. "Now was that so hard?" they asked you.

"Yes," you said. Even as a third grader, you knew how hard it was to create something new in a brain that longs for the familiar.

You discovered that your brain is either super-efficient or lazy. Either way, it requires a great deal of effort to hack your neural way through the jungle of the familiar to plant something unfamiliar.

Your brain is still super-efficient or lazy even though you're no longer a third grader. It begs for the familiar and really tries to exclude anything that is uncharted territory. Your mind's primary function is survival, i.e., to keep you alive. It does not want you to

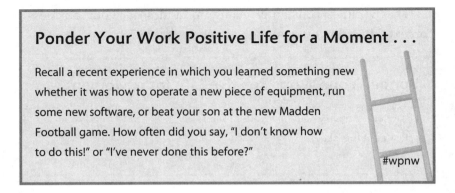

Ponder Your Work Positive Life for a Moment . . .

Recall a recent experience in which you learned something new whether it was how to operate a new piece of equipment, run some new software, or beat your son at the new Madden Football game. How often did you say, "I don't know how to do this!" or "I've never done this before?"

#wpnw

march off the map of previous experiences because that's where danger lurks. It's where the wild things of business are.

So here you are, reading a book titled *Work Positive in a Negative World*, hoping to figure out a way of creating more business success. Most likely, like so many of us, you have become negative about your business, choosing to be like the negative world. Since the world is negative, negativity is familiar. Yes, it's miserable, but nonetheless it is familiar.

You want to change your business (and your life) for some reason, perhaps because what you have always done no longer works for you. You desire different results, positive results, at work. You're praying that there is more to doing business than what you're experiencing. You realize to do business in a different way, you can't keep doing the same old behaviors . . . or else you'll go insane.

Unfortunately your brain does not care whether you are negative or positive about your business. It only longs for the familiar.

So if you choose to perceive negative thoughts about your company or the economy, your mind finds those thoughts familiar. It knows where to file them. It quickly sorts and processes them, pats itself on the back of its cerebrum, and says, "What a good (boy or girl) am I." Your mind loves the familiar, even if it is negative.

So how do you overcome its love of the negative familiar?

Repetition.

That's right, you repeatedly, over and over, choose to perceive the positive about your business and focus your mind on those aspects that, though they may be unfamiliar, are success stories. Just like you did with your multiplication tables, you create some novel neural pathways that over time become familiar.

Who Moved My Coffeemaker?

My wife enjoys rearranging the kitchen counter periodically. She likes to play "spin the kitchen," so she shuffles everything around.

The coffeemakers are moved from one side to the other, which means the canisters with the sugar and flour and stuff are moved to the other side of the stove. And to make room for them, the crock pot and tea maker are repositioned. Of course the napkins get a new location, too.

I make the coffee every evening, programming the brewers to go off the next morning. The first evening I walk in to discover this new arrangement, I naturally go to the previous and familiar location of the coffeemakers and they're not there. So I hunt around the kitchen, find them and begin my preparations, grumbling all the while. The unfamiliar is negative, right?

But then of course the coffee filters, which I had in a drawer near the previous location of the makers, have to be relocated to a closer drawer. Then there's the coffee itself, which previously was stored in a cabinet closest to the "familiar" spot. So the coffee's location has to be changed as well. It took me about 21 evenings to stop walking over to the spot where I made coffee previously and reaching for filters and coffee that were no longer there.

The ways you do business are constantly changing and moving your coffeemaker, aren't they? A new piece of diagnostic equipment is required to do repairs. A more efficient system is introduced into your franchise. A new safety rule is enforced by OSHA. Being a creature of habit, you return to the same spot. Why? Because it is familiar, regardless of whether it was in the best spot or not.

Only through repetition—preparing the coffee every evening for 21 evenings in a row—do we unlearn the familiar and learn the new. That's right—unlearn the familiar and learn the new. It's a two-stage process. Just like we can't simply turn away from the negative aspects of our business when focusing our thoughts, we must also focus on the positive. So it's not just a case of an old dog learning new tricks. The most challenging part of the equation for us old dogs is to unlearn the familiar, clearing room in our minds for a new soon-to-be-familiar trick.

How long did it take me to stop moving to the previous location of the coffeemakers? About three weeks.

Sure I got it right before then. I would get it right three evenings in a row, sometimes four, and then relax. That's when without even thinking about it I stepped over to the coffemaker's previous location. It wasn't until after about 21 evenings that I could do it right unconciously.

How did I finally stop that familiar behavior?

Repetition.

Easier Said Than Done

Think of your perception like a camera. Cameras have different lens functions—panoramic/landscape, normal, and zoom. Odds are if you're old enough to remember Polaroids, if you have a digital camera, you use only one or two functions on it. You have your "standard operating procedure" for taking pictures, which means your camera can do more tricks than you are comfortable trying. Why? You've never done photography this way before—digitally.

Our younger daughter received a new camera for Christmas. It has a far more powerful zoom than any of our others. So one evening I was standing in our kitchen, near the previous location of the coffeemakers, and she was at the table by the bay window. Suddenly, she said, "Daddy, you need to trim your nose hairs."

I look over and from her sitting angle, she had zoomed up and in on my nose. Since she was a teenaged girl at the time consumed with personal hygiene, the status of my nose hairs was of great concern to her lest I go out in public and embarrass her.

Her powerful zoom was great for judging the status of my nose hairs, but when closed in so tightly, prevented her from seeing my eyebrows, eyelashes, and other facial features that I'm sure would have been equally offensive to her. Had she used the landscape/panoramic lens, she would have seen all of me, her mom, the kitchen counter, refrigerator and the rest of the appliances. Yet she could not see them. The zoom was myopic. It created a closed field of vision.

Our minds are set on a default zoom function that perceives the familiar first. It is what we zoom in on. After all, the familiar ways have worked for us in the past and quite well, so why change our field of perception now?

Or, have they? New challenges come each day in business. At first we judge them negatively simply because they are unfamiliar to us. They fail to fit our preconceived notions of how to do some task in our business. We lack categories in which to insert them in

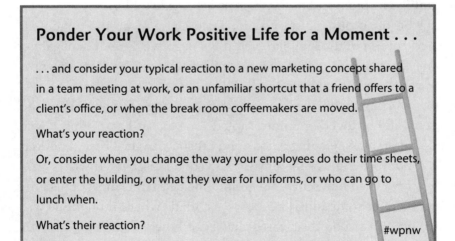

Ponder Your Work Positive Life for a Moment . . .

. . . and consider your typical reaction to a new marketing concept shared in a team meeting at work, or an unfamiliar shortcut that a friend offers to a client's office, or when the break room coffeemakers are moved.

What's your reaction?

Or, consider when you change the way your employees do their time sheets, or enter the building, or what they wear for uniforms, or who can go to lunch when.

What's their reaction?

#wpnw

our brain. So we resist the change, the new, only to wake up the next morning and discover that yesterday's change has been joined by today's change, and tomorrow's change lurks in the shadows, ready to pop out when the clock strikes midnight.

The mantra "I've never done it this way before" is absolutely true. Redefining the reality of this statement from one of resistance to change to one that is followed by "That's right, and if I don't want to go broke, I'd better learn how to do it this way as quickly as possible" is absolutely critical if you're going to continue to be in business today, much less enjoy a work positive lifestyle.

So What Is Your Typical Reaction to Something Unfamiliar?

Be honest, and remember: Your brain is super-efficient and basically lazy.

Your mind perceives the familiar first and longs for it, even if it is negative.

You avoid thinking familiar, negative thoughts only through repetitive reprogramming of your mind to search out the positive aspects of your business, zoom in on them, and hold your focus until your brain stubbornly creates a new file folder.

So often our typical reaction is to chase away the unfamiliar and cocoon in the familiar even if it's negative. Sure it is negative, maybe even miserable, but it is familiar. But there are consequences if you remain in the familiar.

Our family enjoyed an extended weekend at the beach, just to relax and be together uninterrupted. One day as I sat with my wife and daughters, reading a book and relishing in the ocean, I noticed a sandpiper. He was by himself, and soon I discovered why.

I watched him scurrying around the beach like most of his type looking for something to eat. At least that's what I thought he was doing. But I soon discovered that's not how he spent most of his time. That sandpiper used most of his time and energy to chase away other birds. If another sandpiper approached his territory, he quickly ran over to chase him off. Then another bird invaded the opposite end of his area and he was off to chase her away. Back and forth that little bird ran, spending virtually no time eating and all his energy chasing away the competition.

Do you spend most of your daily mental energy at work defending your familiar turf, chasing away any change or unfamiliar thoughts just like this paranoid sandpiper who perceives that there isn't enough food to go around?

Remember: Before the old dog can learn new tricks, he must unlearn the old ones, creating room in his mind for the unfamiliar. So must the sandpiper. And so must you and I.

There is a cumulative effect on your life if you remain locked up mentally in only the familiar. Look around at the abandoned buildings that once housed businesses in your region. They're locked now, but the mental lock-up by the business owner took place long before the real estate was. While some familiar thoughts continue to serve you well, there are others—in fact, most of them— that don't. You have never done business in a market exactly like this before.

For some of us, it's like being a teenager again, an uncontrollable tsunami of economic hormones washing over your brain. If you're a first-time entrepreneur, this is your first experience out on your own, paying the lease and buying supplies and getting up on your own to go to your business, not just a job. If you've been in business for a while, it's like being middle-aged—you're wearing glasses for the first time just to read your P&L and discovering that your net profit is redistributing in places you don't like. If you're a mature business owner, you wake up each morning to a new ache or pain in your marketing plan—"Why should I put my 'Face' on a 'Book' and I thought birds tweeted"—and the constant yet unfamiliar reality that you physically can't do what you've always done without getting tired, but have to because you cut payroll expenses.

While some of the familiar thoughts we nurture can serve us well, we do well to apply that disclaimer we hear in all the financial services companies' ads: Our past success is no guarantee of future performance. Business changes daily just like the financial markets. The mercurial essence of doing business today slips in and away, it ebbs and flows; no two days are exactly alike, despite what our brains would tell us.

It's this reality that makes it absolutely critical for you to avoid focusing only on familiar thoughts, to redefine the reality in your head, to welcome novelty into your perceptions; through repetition to create new neural pathways and categories in your mind that release that jet fuel of imagination to soar into the stratosphere of positivity that fulfills your business goals and makes your dreams come true. You search out the positive in your business, learn positive practices from similar and dissimilar industries and adapt them, despite any unfamiliarity, and cognitively embrace them so you can work positive.

How do you avoid perceiving just familiar thoughts, which are often negative because they don't work, and welcome unfamiliar ones?

Embracing the Unfamiliar

Repeatedly perceive the unfamiliar, intentionally choosing to suspend judgment in pursuit of the positive. Through repetition, you force your brain to form new categories and file the positive until it becomes familiar. You implement this newly familiar positive in your business and discover new revenue streams, new markets, new customers, and most of all, a new satisfaction for why you do what you do. You work positive.

Here's how it works. My wife received some new horses to board that came from a farm about 2,000 miles away. The previous farm was set up differently than ours. The horses were in a much smaller area. In fact, these four horses daily walked a space that measured about 100 feet by 100 feet. So when my wife put these horses into a five-acre pasture, you would think that the first thing they would do would be to run all over it, happy to be in a significantly larger space, right?

At first, the largest horse, who happened to be the leader of his herd, stood basically in one spot all day. In his mind, he was still enclosed in a very small space even though he had all the five-acre pasture to enjoy. He didn't move.

When he did move a few days later, he walked a perimeter that measured 100 feet by 100 feet—the same size space he occupied previously. He was still a prisoner in his mind of the small space. Even though he was unhappy, even miserable to the point of biting the other horses while in that small space, he could not escape his familiar patterns.

The interesting thing to me was to watch him gently begin to explore our larger pasture. Only gradually did his mental picture of where he could spend the day expand to include all the new, unfamiliar five-acre pasture. Repeatedly, he walked the previous space. Then bit by bit, he expanded his space to include part of the unfamiliar pasture. Through repetition, he became more and more comfortable with more space.

After about 21 days of this tentative exploration, he burst into a gallop and surged through the pasture with reckless abandon, kicking up his heels, toward the fence line at the far end of the five acres. When he arrived at the fence, he just stood there for a moment, admiring the view. Then he turned to look back at where he had been, nickered to the other three horses, and they galloped to where he stood.

Your brain is super-efficient and lazy.

Your mind perceives the familiar first and longs for it, even if it is negative.

You avoid thinking familiar, negative thoughts only through repetitive reprogramming of your mind.

If a horse can do it, so can you.

Ponder Your Work Positive Life for a Moment . . .

. . . and relive an experience in which you faced a change in your business—large or small—and eventually, through repeated efforts, successfully navigated it.

Put yourself back into the struggle of the change, but also revel in the sense of achievement and elation as you positively emerged on the other side. Remember the additional revenue you generated. Recall your customers' faces as you provided a new solution to their problems. Relive your employees' looks as "your change" actually worked. What was that like?

#wpnw

Who Moved My Furniture?

I painted our master bedroom. My wife decided it was a great time to rearrange the furniture in the room. (You see a pattern here, don't you?) It was OK by me. I like change . . . until I got up in the middle of the night the first night it was rearranged and bumped into a chair that wasn't there before. I almost didn't make it to the bathroom.

Then the second night I stubbed my little toe on a dresser. I sat down in the floor just to make sure it wasn't bleeding profusely, wondering, "How can something so small hurt so big?"

The third night I tried to knock off the little toe on the other foot on the footboard of our bed. Of course, I was protecting the previously injured little toe. This time, I was down on my hands and knees, crawling around the bedroom, searching for my toe which I knew I had knocked off; praying it could be surgically reattached.

On the fourth night, I decided that perhaps I would do well to wake up and look where I was going. I didn't want to turn on a light and wake my wife. So I started peering into the darkness more . . .

. . . and discovered that the dark really isn't so dark. The area light in a nearby horse pasture streams in through a window and lights part of my path. Later I discovered that on a night when there's a full moon, one portion of the room is literally bathed in light; so bright I can see quite well.

Sometimes your life at work seems dark—as in red ink, not black—because you perceived only the familiar and that's led to negative injuries. It's in that moment of discovery that you find there is more light in your business than you previously imagined; that you can peer into the dark shadows and find just enough unfamiliar positivity for your journey so you can travel safely through the treacherous waters of both black and red ink.

When you make this discovery, when you perceive an unfamiliar, positive thought and your negative begins to lighten, repeat it.

Do it again.

And again.

And again.

Avoid only familiar thoughts.

Perceive unfamiliar thoughts.

Then celebrate, because you've just taken another step in your journey toward your work positive lifestyle in business, discovering how you can make a positive life, not just a living, while doing business in a negative world.

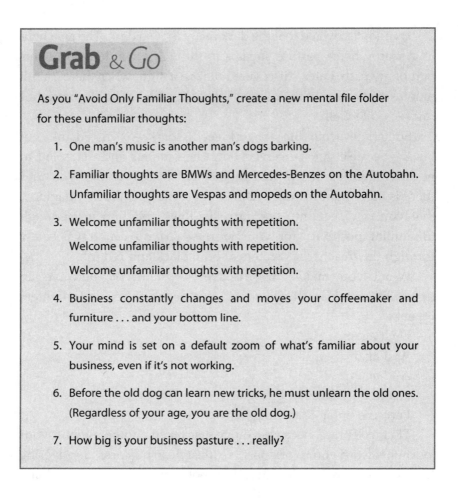

Grab & Go

As you "Avoid Only Familiar Thoughts," create a new mental file folder for these unfamiliar thoughts:

1. One man's music is another man's dogs barking.

2. Familiar thoughts are BMWs and Mercedes-Benzes on the Autobahn. Unfamiliar thoughts are Vespas and mopeds on the Autobahn.

3. Welcome unfamiliar thoughts with repetition.

    Welcome unfamiliar thoughts with repetition.

    Welcome unfamiliar thoughts with repetition.

4. Business constantly changes and moves your coffeemaker and furniture . . . and your bottom line.

5. Your mind is set on a default zoom of what's familiar about your business, even if it's not working.

6. Before the old dog can learn new tricks, he must unlearn the old ones. (Regardless of your age, you are the old dog.)

7. How big is your business pasture . . . really?

CHAPTER 4

Filter Your Thoughts

"You must not under any pretense allow your mind
to dwell on any thought that is not positive,
constructive, optimistic, kind."

—Emmet Fox

Let me be completely honest with you. I work for my wife.
Literally.

This small farm we live on? She runs it. She directs the care of the horses and the yellow Labrador retrievers she raises. But I work for her in taking care of all the other stuff.

I love working for her. I coach business people and travel to do speaking engagements in which I stimulate individuals and organizations to listen to life and make a work positive life in this negative world. I make decisions all the time in leading my companies. So it is really nice for me to just do what she tells me to do on the farm. Also, it helps me stay married to my college sweetheart.

Another part of the attraction is she lets me play with power tools. Like chainsaws and weed trimmers and saws and drills and other things that make lots of noise and smell like gas and oil.

She gave me a mission one day—clear the brush from under the electric fence. The brush grows up underneath it, touches the wire, and reduces the electrical shock that keeps the horses in the pasture.

So off I went, chainsaw and weed trimmer in hand, hacking away at all this undergrowth attacking our fence line. As I worked along, I noticed a sapling growing right under the fence line. I reached for my chainsaw, and just before cranking it, looked back at the sapling and studied its leaves. It was a maple sapling, the kind of tree that blazes orange in the fall, appearing to be on fire in the sunlight, the type of tree that I think is absolutely beautiful.

You see, I grew up in a part of the world where pine trees grow like weeds. Pine trees look the same all year long. Hardwoods like maples are rare in that area. Even after all these years of being gone, maples in the fall are a novelty to me.

I put the chainsaw down and picked up my shovel. I would dig up the maple sapling and transplant it to another place on the farm where I could enjoy its beauty. So I aimed my shovel at the sapling, and just then noticed something growing beside it—poison ivy.

Have you ever touched poison ivy? It causes a miserable itch that lasts for weeks, making you scratch yourself in embarrassing places while in public. I did not want poison ivy on me or my shovel.

So I stood there, thinking about what to do next, when it hit me—there they were: irritating poison ivy and a maple tree destined to be 35 feet tall and blaze orange in the fall growing in the same soil, side by side. Something beautiful growing right beside something ugly. The best in nature nurtured next to the worst. Something that causes me to praise nature is nestled alongside something to curse about it.

Just doesn't seem right, does it? At least that's what I was thinking.

Then I realized that the soil really did not care what's planted in it—a maple tree or poison ivy. The soil nourishes and grows whatever it receives.

Your Mind Is Like Soil

You can choose to plant poison ivy—only familiar, negative thoughts that erupt in itches of worry that cause economic scratching. Or, you can choose to plant maple trees—unfamiliar, positive thoughts like fascination with new best business practices. Your mind nourishes and grows whatever it receives.

Your first step to a work positive lifestyle is choosing to perceive the positive in the world around you. Your mind focuses your thoughts every second, and you now know the importance of aiming that focus on the positive in your business. Your mind craves the familiar, even if it is negative, and you now understand how to carve out new neural pathways in your super-efficient yet lazy brain.

The third key aspect of perceiving the positive in the world around you as you do business is to filter your thoughts. When you focus your thoughts, you turn away from the negative and toward the positive. When you avoid too familiar thoughts, you search out unfamiliar thoughts. The reality of doing business today is that sometimes you turn away from a negative thought and run right into another one. You keep turning, only to discover that you are surrounded by negativity. And sometimes as you avoid just familiar thoughts, you bump into so many familiar thoughts that you wonder how you will find your way out into the Land of Unfamiliar.

What do you do then?

You filter your thoughts.

Filters Keep Some Things Out and Let Other Things Pass Through

Consider your office's heating and air conditioning system. It has a filter that keeps dust out and lets air in. Think about your car's air filter. It catches road dirt and allows the air to pass cleanly so it can mix with the gasoline and power your car. I have a water filter on our home's well. The minerals are caught and the water flows through.

Filters don't deny the existence of dust and dirt and minerals. They counteract them, holding them at bay, until the filter becomes full or clogged and someone changes it out for a fresh one.

As you filter your thoughts, you direct your mind in the same way. There is way too much negativity in the world to deny its existence. Bad things happen to good businesses every day, and just as perplexing is the reality that good things happen to bad businesses daily. To deny that the world is largely negative is Pollyanna at best and psychotic at worst. Our own stumbling-around efforts at discovering how to work positive prove that.

My wife's best friend gave my wife a wine glass with this saying painted on it: "Lead me not into temptation . . . I can find it on my own." The same can be said of negativity. We can't deny the reality of the negative in the world because we know its physical address. No GPS is required to locate 1313 Negative Lane.

That's why the work positive business lifestyle you want is all about how to be positive even in a negative economic environment. That's also why you filter your thoughts rather than deny the existence of negativity in the world around you.

Ponder Your Work Positive Life for a Moment . . .

Name a recent experience in which you found yourself in a negative conversation at work and joined in by adding to the already downward spiraling talk.

What were you thinking or how were you feeling as you walked away?

#wpnw

What You Resist, Persists

There is an old saying, "What you resist, persists." That is, when you focus your thoughts on not being negative, you concentrate on the negative. For example, when you tell yourself, "Now don't forget to . . ." your mind zeroes in on the word "forget." And what do you usually do? Forget it. When you tell yourself, "Now remember to . . ." your mind takes aim at the word "remember." And what do you usually do? Remember it. It's not a denial of the negative. It's a filtering of the negative in order to affirm the positive. By resisting, you focus on the negative. By filtering it, you acknowledge it and choose the more positive.

My friend, Bob Nicoll, tells the story of walking into a convenience store one hot summer day in Phoenix and seeing a sign above the cash register, "Don't Forget the Ice." He asked the manager how his ice sales were. "Slow," the manager said, despite the fact that it was about 110 degrees in the shade.

So Bob asked for a piece of paper and a magic marker. He created another sign that read, "Remember the Ice." He asked the manager to remove the current sign, put up the new one, and see if that helped sales.

When Bob returned to the store in about three weeks, the manager was so excited to see him. "I've tripled my sales of bags of ice," he said. "And it's all due to your great sign! Thank you!" (Go to www.RemembertheIce.com to discover more.)

What you resist, persists. Poison ivy grows in your business. We all have customers, clients, and employees who irritate us. These poison ivy relationships grow in the same soil as your maple tree relationships. You filter out the poison ivy by refusing to plant it, and when it does grow, by uprooting it—which is what I did that day on our farm—and choosing instead to plant and nurture the maple trees.

Let me give you an example of how filtering your thoughts to keep out the negative and let the positive pass through works. Tons of sand and dirt were being moved at the beach while my family and I were on vacation. A company was replenishing the beach front with sand from the ocean floor because a hurricane had eroded it. Pumping in tons of dirt from the ocean floor made the shallow shore water murky and dirty-looking.

Our younger daughter and I went down to check out the water. It was so muddy you couldn't see your feet or anything else even in the shallow water. It was so muddy that I said to our daughter, who was about 5 years old at the time, "Yuck! Look how dirty the ocean is."

She said to me, "But Daddy, it looks like a chocolate ocean to me."

I looked down at the water again, and this time I saw it. The water really did look chocolate brown. I almost wanted to get down on my hands and knees and drink it up.

My daughter and I looked at the same ocean water, but with two entirely different perspectives. I saw, "Yuck!" She saw, "Yum!"

She filtered out the obvious, perceiving beyond it, to discover the positive.

You have a choice about what you perceive in your business— yuck or yum. Positive or negative. Your mind will grow either you choose. You filter according to what you choose to enjoy in your work positive lifestyle.

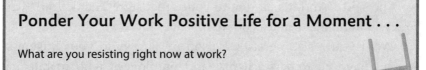

Ponder Your Work Positive Life for a Moment . . .

What are you resisting right now at work?

Be surgically honest as you think about it.

#wpnw

Clean Your Filter

A woman and her husband sat at the kitchen table each morning, drinking their coffee and eating their breakfast. One morning, the husband noticed the neighbor's laundry hung out to dry. "Boy," he said, "she sure doesn't know how to wash clothes. They're still dirty." The wife glanced out the window, but said nothing.

The next week, they sat down at the breakfast table again and this time he said, "Well, she learned how to wash clothes. They're bright and clean. Did you say something to her?"

"No, I didn't," said the wife. "But I did clean that window."

Sometimes our filters on the world get clogged or dirty, and they require cleaning for us to have an accurate read on what's positive and what's negative in our businesses. When we are stuck in the familiar negative, and refuse to filter it, we immediately develop a rather critical view of other people and situations. Our perception is blurred, much like my vision was in fourth grade when playing baseball and trying to read math problems. We begin criticizing our employees for coming in a few minutes late, forgetting they worked over the night before.

One way to clear up this blurring of our perception is to change our perspective. When we change our perspective, we unclog the filter of our thoughts. I learned the value of a new perspective which unclogs this filter as I painted the board fencing on our farm. I bought a five-gallon bucket of stain and lugged it up and down the fence line as I smeared it with my four-inch brush.

Section by section, I painted one side of the fence, and then went to the other side. At one section, there wasn't a gate close by and I really didn't want to carry that heavy bucket up the hill to the gate. So I came up with the brilliant idea of lifting the bucket up over the fence, putting it down on the other side, and then climbing over the fence myself. Sounds easy enough, right?

Well, I got the heavy bucket over the top board of the fence, but then as it got closer to the ground on the other side and as I stretched further and further to let it down, I tipped it and spilled stain on the ground. I wasn't very pleased with myself. OK, I was angry.

I climbed over the fence, and looked at the mess I'd made, wondering why I couldn't have held the bucket more firmly until it touched the ground. Just then, from my new perspective on the other side of the fence, I noticed that the bottom of the fence was high enough for me to have slid the bucket under the fence instead of lifting it over.

You can imagine what I was thinking—"I wish I had a second chance to do that over."

Do you ever wish for a second chance?

Sure you do. You do something. The results are different from what you wanted. You get a new perspective on it and realize what you could have done. Then you want a second chance. You want to unclog your perception filter.

A Great Thing about Your Work Positive Lifestyle

One of the great things about choosing to enjoy a work positive lifestyle in your business is that you discover "do-overs." The mistakes you make deciphering the success code of your business are an expected part of your learning curve. You have an experience like mine. You learn something from a new perspective that helps you unstop your filter. Then you find yourself in a similar situation and you do it over, this time with the benefit of what you learned previously. It's a do-over, just like me while painting the fence. What do you think I did the next time I was far away from a gate? I checked out which was better—lift the bucket over the fence or slide it under.

You filter your thoughts, reflecting on previous work experiences and what you can learn from them, and that determines what you allow to pass through your filter—the positive—and what you filter out—the negative.

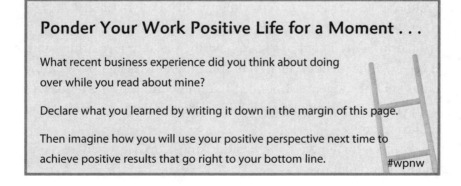

Ponder Your Work Positive Life for a Moment . . .

What recent business experience did you think about doing over while you read about mine?

Declare what you learned by writing it down in the margin of this page.

Then imagine how you will use your positive perspective next time to achieve positive results that go right to your bottom line.

#wpnw

Filtering in Reverse

So often, rather than filtering our perceptions in this way, we allow the negative world to make our decisions for us, to color our attitudes in dark hues of economic depression and financial doom. The world gives us a filter that's the reversal of the positive life you want to achieve through your business.

For instance, it's a rainy Monday. Now what's your typical attitude toward such a day? "No customers will come in today in this kind of weather," you think.

You could just as easily perceive, "The customers who walk through my door today are ready to buy if they'll come out in this weather."

Now, what if your area is experiencing a drought? What's your attitude?

But what if the drought has made the ground hard and the rain is falling so forcefully that it's simply sheeting off, without a real chance for the ground to absorb it? What's your attitude now?

"I bet we'll have a flash flood watch declared and nobody will come in."

But what would a child see on such a rainy Monday?

- Mud puddles to play in.
- Rivers to stand in and watch the water splash up your legs.
- Boat races with leaves and twigs.
- Bathwater for birds.
- "Can I go fishing?"
- The flowers and grass and trees getting watered.

See how filtering your thoughts makes a positive change in how you perceive the world around you in which you're doing business?

What if you allow negative thoughts to pass through and enter your mind without filtering? What happens to your company then?

Imagine with me for a moment that before you start your car or truck each morning to go to work that you put six grains of sand in your gas tank.

OK, it's only six grains of sand, but if you do it every morning, how long do you think it'll take before your vehicle won't run? Soon, right? That great engine would be a mess, unable to do what it was designed to do.

Negative, unpleasant thoughts dropped into your mind affect you in the same way. They break down your mental motor. You're broken down by worry, frustration, and thoughts that your business doesn't matter to anyone. Pretty soon, you're broken down beside the business fast lane and you can't go on.

When you filter your thoughts, you prevent such tiny grains of negativity from entering your mental engine. You selectively leave them out, not resisting them, but proactively selecting to avoid allowing them to come inside and play in your business.

Some friends came over to our farm for the first time. The weather was warm enough so that my roses were still blooming. As we walked around, one of our friends said, "Your roses are so beautiful! They are gorgeous. I wish I could grow roses."

I realized that to someone who doesn't grow roses, they really were beautiful. But when I looked at them, I saw the black spot fungus growing on the leaves, turning them yellow, and making them drop off. When I looked at them, I saw the stunted growth of the canes, stunted because of the drought going on at the time. When I looked at them, I saw what was wrong with the rose bushes, looking right past the beautiful blooms.

The same thing happens as you perceive your company. You can filter out the negative and look at the beautiful experiences blossoming all around your business. The opportunities popping up almost overnight. The resources converging that you imagined. Or, you can bring an unfiltered perception to all the things going wrong with your business and the environment around it. The tight credit market. The economic slowdown. The high jobless rate.

When you filter out the negative perceptions about your business, you choose a positive path to success.

CHAPTER 5

"I Conceive"

"I think positive. I always think we're going to score. Two minutes is a lot of time if you have timeouts and you're throwing every down. I've always had great receivers, which helps. It's not just me doing it."

—Dan Marino

You have begun the first step to your work positive lifestyle— "I PERCEIVE the POSITIVE at work." You discovered that your mind naturally focuses, that it prefers to focus on the familiar, but that you can choose to focus on the unfamiliar and filter your thoughts to fill your mind and business with the positive.

If you're like me, once I'm filling my mind with positive thoughts, I like to share those with someone else. I want to check with another person—for confirmation, validation, and expansion of the positive thoughts.

Such a desire is natural. We are created social beings, not existential isolationists. In fact, we often uncover hidden sources of positivity with others.

Usually my wife cares for the horses on our farm, but on one particular occasion she was out of town. I was home so I volunteered to feed the horses.

By the time I got home from my office, nightfall had arrived, and it was an extremely dark night. There was no moon. It was cloudy and the sky held no visible stars. Also, the area light needed a new bulb, something I'd intended to do for a few weeks.

I poured the feed into the buckets in the barn and headed for the pasture gate. This group of horses is fed outside, not in the barn, in black pails on the ground. Sometimes they play with their black pails and roll them around the pasture.

I stepped through the gate, hooked it behind me, and started looking for those black pails on a black night. So here I am, looking for black pails on the ground on an extremely dark night when the horses hear me muttering to myself, "Now where are those pails? And why isn't there any light out here?" They know my presence means feeding time so they gallop up beside me, not understanding why I don't just put the feed in the pails and get out of their way.

So here I am on a black night looking for black pails, being jostled by horses who just want to eat. I started dancing around the pasture, trying to keep the horses from stepping on my feet, which of course means they started dancing around trying not to step on my feet.

I thought to myself, "Instead of stumbling around the pasture with horses chasing you for feed, let the horses show you where the pails are."

I stopped my dancing, stood perfectly still, and told the horses to "Go on." Then I watched as they went and stood in various places around the pasture. I walked up to each one and discovered a black pail on the ground in front of them, poured in the feed, and moved on to the next one. The horses could see the pails when I couldn't. I let them guide me.

Do you ever find yourself stumbling around in the negative darkness of your business for something positive? Even though you have taken the first step of perceiving your work positive lifestyle, sometimes you still need some help conceiving your perception.

Yes, you can see it, but you can benefit from someone else's conceptions—their experiences, knowledge, and network.

Such was the case with me and the horses. Sure, I had the feed they wanted, but I didn't know how best to deliver it to them. They knew how the feed was to be delivered. I partnered with the horses, and together we achieved their feeding.

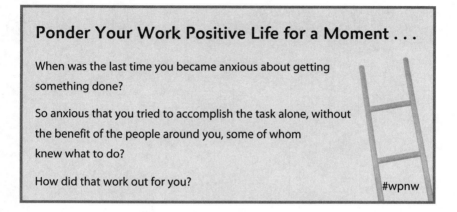

Ponder Your Work Positive Life for a Moment . . .

When was the last time you became anxious about getting something done?

So anxious that you tried to accomplish the task alone, without the benefit of the people around you, some of whom knew what to do?

How did that work out for you?

#wpnw

The second step to enjoying a work positive lifestyle, once you perceive it, is to conceive the positive in your business. Conception is not something you can do alone. It takes two. Think of conceiving the positive at work as the social dynamic of enjoying your work positive lifestyle.

CHAPTER 6

Cooperate Completely

"Great discoveries and improvements invariably involve the cooperation of many minds. I may be given credit for having blazed the trail, but when I look at the subsequent developments I feel the credit is due to others rather than to myself."

—Alexander Graham Bell

You were created to work positive with others.

Your business success depends on you attracting customers or clients and employees with whom you conceive a work positive lifestyle. Your first step in this direction, having focused and filtered positive perceptions and embraced unfamiliar, positive thoughts, is to conceive the positive by cooperating completely.

Such cooperation challenges the familiar notions of achieving positive success by becoming a self-made person and pulling yourself up by your own bootstraps. Despite its familiarity, such a notion is simply a myth. You've been the beneficiary of conceiving your positive lifestyle with others since before you can remember.

Do you remember your mother and father getting up at two o'clock in the morning to feed you? You're thinking about getting up to feed your child at two o'clock in the morning. I asked you if you remember when you were an infant lying in a crib, screaming your head off because your stomach is growling, and all of a sudden, this bleary-eyed person appears over your crib, reaches down, picks you up, and holds you close. You feel the warmth of that embrace. You hear a soft voice. You are fed. The next thing you know, you fall asleep again, back in your crib, totally satisfied and happy. Do you remember that experience?

Of course not. Even though it happened night after night for months and months, depriving your parents of much-needed sleep, these gracious acts of compassionate kindness your parents offered just because they loved you slip through your memory.

Despite your lack of remembering them, they still happened. There are other gracious acts of cooperation others have done for you that similarly slip through. Some of them were done without your knowledge. Prayers offered for your safety as you drove away from your home for the first time. A diaper changed. A sippy cup of juice poured. Long hours worked to buy you new jeans or pay your car insurance.

All of these completely cooperative acts combine to make you who you are today—a wonderful, unique human being capable of a work positive lifestyle.

However alone you may feel at times in your business, someone is with you. You were created to be in cooperative relationships with others. You have not arrived at your current life's mile marker as a solo driver. You have traveled in a carpool the whole time.

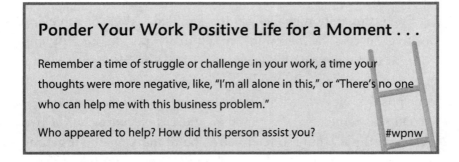

Ponder Your Work Positive Life for a Moment . . .

Remember a time of struggle or challenge in your work, a time your thoughts were more negative, like, "I'm all alone in this," or "There's no one who can help me with this business problem."

Who appeared to help? How did this person assist you?   #wpnw

Who Do You Lean On?

In our yard was a stand of pines. Their limbs had grown together. Also in our yard was one pine growing by itself.

A snowfall came and the ice and snow lay heavy on the branches of those pines, so heavy that the weight bent their branches down toward the ground, so low in fact that in the stand of pines, the branches from one tree were on the trunk and branches of another, but none of the branches broke because the trees leaned their branches on one another.

The pine that stood by itself didn't do as well. There were no other trees to lean against so the lone pine's branches became so heavy they broke.

Together we're stronger and live longer than any one of us by ourselves. The people around you—customers/clients, employees/employers, family/friends, and vendors/suppliers—are there for you to lean on when the weight of doing business is too much for you to stand alone . . . and when isn't it? These people are your team. I like to think of these people as "Team Joey."

You were created to cooperate with others.

I discovered the creative nature of our conceiving relationships as I pulled up to a bank drive-in and found an open lane. It was my first time using this bank's drive-through service. I'm accustomed to the ones that have the round container that open at one end, you throw your stuff in, close it, place it back on the tube, and push the button.

This one was different. It had a blue box and no buttons. Well, the box I figured out and placed it back on the tube. The sign read, "Autoconveyor" so I thought you just put it back and away it goes. I placed the box back, but nothing happened.

I looked at the person in the vehicle beside me, smiled, and hoped they didn't see what I couldn't do. I mean, it's kind of embarrassing, especially for a guy, not to know how to operate machinery.

Just then, a voice came on the intercom and said, "Please push the box up a little." I did and away it went as I laughed at myself and my concern over who was watching.

We all require a little help occasionally. For you to conceive your work life as positive, you reach out for a little help from your friends. Sometimes you get it whether you reach out or not.

A couple arrived at an automobile dealership to pick up their car. They were told that the keys had been locked accidentally in it. So they went to the service department and found a mechanic working feverishly to unlock the driver's side door.

As the wife watched from the passenger's side door, she instinctively tried the door handle and discovered it was open. "Hey," she told the mechanic, "it's open!"

"I know," he answered, "I already got that side."

This mechanic obviously got so involved in his task that he lost sight of the big picture—getting into the car. He needed some help to regain his perspective.

Can you relate?

Ponder Your Work Positive Life for a Moment . . .

When was the last time you got so involved in a work task that you lost sight of the big picture? Did someone come along and help you regain your positive perception of life? How did this person cooperate with you to conceive the positive?

#wpnw

Something You Miss

Cooperating completely with others presupposes that you know partially; that you are incomplete alone, but complete with others. Sometimes, our ego gets in the way of conceiving a work positive lifestyle. Part of the challenge for entrepreneurs is that we are really good at so many and varied tasks that we buy the lie that we can truly do it all. The truth is that if we passionately want to make our dreams come true, we must redefine our egotistical reality of "I can do it all" to "There is something I missed."

One day a blue block of frozen material crashed from the sky into a farmer's field. He cut off a chunk of it, put it in his freezer, and called the sheriff. He was convinced it was something extraterrestrial, but all he really knew was it stunk when it melted.

The sheriff examined it and didn't have a clue, so he called a chemistry professor from the local college. The professor took a sample from it and left with the promise to analyze it in her lab and call back with the results. The farmer kept the blue frozen material in his freezer, making sure that it was carefully preserved. He just knew he had discovered the key to life in an alien universe.

The chemistry professor called the farmer. "Sir," she said, "your blue frozen material is definitely not extraterrestrial so you can relax. But please take it out of your freezer and throw it away as soon as possible."

"Why?" the farmer asked.

"Because, sir," she said, "what you have in your freezer is the portable toilet fluid ejected from a plane as it flew over your farm."

One of the most essential ingredients of our cooperative conceiving of the work positive lifestyle is that no matter how much you perceive, and think you perceive accurately in life, there is something you miss—or some subject that someone else knows more about than you do. Just like the chemistry professor and the farmer . . .

And then there was the man who was flying along in a single engine airplane and the engine stalled. He couldn't get it going again and the plane was diving to crash very quickly. He couldn't pull it up so he strapped on a parachute and jumped out of the plane.

Well, to make matters worse, the parachute wouldn't open no matter how hard he pulled on the ripcord. He was frantic and considered what to do as he plunged to what he knew would be his death.

He looked down, and all of a sudden saw a man flying up towards him from the ground. So here the two men are in the air, passing each other; the pilot headed down and the other man headed up. The pilot with the broken parachute yelled at the man headed up, "Do you know anything about fixing parachutes?"

"No," the man yelled back. "Do you know anything about fixing gas furnaces?"

No matter which direction your business is going—up or down—you can use some help. The good news is you have it. The universe is designed to partner with you, to provide resources beyond your control for your business's well-being. You are in relationships with others and the world around you to receive everything you require to work positive.

Think about the Wildflowers

I have a friend who worked in the family business for most of his adult life. Sure he operated as a business owner, but his father started the business. It was his father who spent sleepless nights worrying about making payroll and whether his suppliers would extend credit again. My friend was insulated from such anxieties . . . until the family business was sold, and he started his own business. He became an entrepreneur really for the first time. Over lunch one day, he talked about being on the "front line" of his business, from the ground up, and the pressures he was enduring. Particularly troublesome for him was what he called "financial terror." You and I know it as the compilation of concerns about cash flow, credit, profit margins, etc. Not knowing if there would be enough to support his family in the lifestyle to which they were accustomed kept him up late at night and woke him each morning.

As a business owner, I told him that I can relate with his "financial terror." He asked me, "How do you deal with it?"

I told him about the daylilies growing in beds near our home and along the driveway. Through drought and monsoon, they just keep growing and even show up in places where I didn't plant them. I really don't do much for them except keep as many weeds away as I can. They have continued to grow without my really caring for them.

They are absolutely beautiful! Their orange and yellow and maroon and pink colors make outstanding borders around the horse pastures and driveways. About all I do is transplant a few in the fall.

Then I told him about all the varieties of birds with whom my wife and I share our farm. There are bluebirds, geese, crows, goldfinches, hawks, owls, wrens, sparrows, cardinals, blue jays, mockingbirds, whippoorwills, swallows, martins, woodpeckers, and the list goes on. We feed them in the winter when the snow covers the ground. They eat the mosquitoes and other bugs that would drive us indoors in the spring. Their songs greet us in the mornings, carry us through the days, and put us to bed at night. We do very little for them and yet they brighten our world.

I told him that it seems to me that if the universe's design includes the care of daylilies and birds, it seems logically consistent and even appropriate that everything we need to work positive is there waiting for us.

There really is enough to go around.

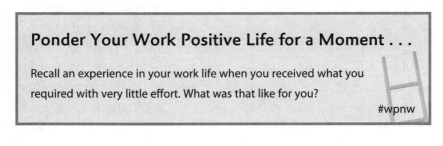

Ponder Your Work Positive Life for a Moment . . .

Recall an experience in your work life when you received what you required with very little effort. What was that like for you?

#wpnw

Who Do You Attract?

Conceiving your work positive lifestyle consists of more than just your efforts alone that generate positivity. You are in relationships already that validate, confirm, and even expand your perception of how you can work positive. You literally were born into these relationships, created to cooperate completely both with the universe and those in it with you. Living into these relationships is the key to conceiving your work positive life.

The key to leveraging these relationships is to focus and filter your perceptions in such a way that you become the kind of person that you want to attract into your business life. You become the person that is like the persons you want to do business with as customers/clients, employees/employers, and vendors/suppliers.

Consider these questions in shaping yourself to conceive your work positive life with positive partners:

1. What are my core values, i.e., those character traits that I want to exhibit in my business relationships? What would my family members say are my core values?
2. What are my life priorities, i.e., those matters in life that I consider most important not just in word, but in work behavior as well? How do my calendar and bank statement reflect these priorities?
3. What is my unique contribution to make in the world through my business and how do I live into it daily?

Just as "birds of a feather flock together," so you literally attract people with whom you share core values and life priorities, and those to whom you contribute uniquely. This attraction factor is a key determiner of how you conceive a work positive lifestyle with others, team members and customers alike. By focusing on and filtering your perceptions, you choose how you work positive. Your business and how you work positive are the magnetic predispositions for selecting those people with whom you conceive.

For example, if you conceive your business more positively and root it therein because you choose to focus and filter in this way, you attract similarly dispositioned people. Those who resonate on this frequency are literally drawn to you because of your common business life pitch.

Conversely, if your business life is more negatively grounded, you find people coming into your business—whether as customers/ clients, employees/suppliers—who are more of a negative persuasion. They vibrate on a negative pitch and are drawn to you on that frequency.

You are created to cooperate. You resemble those with whom you share common core values and life priorities who will receive your unique contribution whether as customers, employees, or vendors. Again, your work life pitch and how it is tuned broadcasts vibrations that resonate with similarly strung persons.

Do you ever find yourself complaining about your customers? They don't pay their bills on time, or maybe they're constantly trying to get something for nothing. Who attracted them to your business?

What about your employees? Ever hear yourself saying something like, "You just can't find good help these days" or "Nobody wants to want work anymore"? Who hired these employees?

Think about your suppliers or vendors or franchiser for a moment. Do you refer to them as ". . . always having a hand in your pocket" or ". . . wouldn't cross the street to help me if my business was bleeding"? Who chose to do business with these people?

Now stop, and ask yourself: "How am I attracting these people? What is there about me that attracts them, that pitches them in my direction?"

One of the greatest challenges in understanding how to conceive a work positive lifestyle is understanding that like attracts like. These people onto whom you shift responsibility for your challenges are in your work life because you chose them. You attracted them by way of your business's core values, your business priorities, and your business's unique contribution.

Once you perceive your work life as positive, then, because you are created to cooperate completely, you begin to attract others to your team who share your positive direction. Those who choose to work positive find their way to you.

In 1948, Boston University and a research team began a heart disease project searching for indicators that predict heart attacks. Over 12,000 persons from three generations have participated. The results are fascinating not only in predicting heart attacks, but also in proving the undeniable nature of how you attract others.

Obesity is a direct correlative to heart attacks. The Framingham Heart Study found that obese people attract each other, and that if you are not obese, but associate with obese persons, you are about 171 percent more likely to become obese yourself.

Think about it. Associating with individuals who have unhealthy eating habits creates the context in which your nutrition behavior changes. The attraction factor not only draws those with whom you share similar traits, it changes the physical characteristics of those attracted.

Divorce is a major life stressor. Researchers studying the effects of divorce on heart attacks also discovered that if you socially associate with mostly divorced persons, you are about 147 percent more likely to divorce yourself.

Think about it. If you work in an office with people who chronically complain about their spouses, or ex-spouses, pretty soon your view of your spouse becomes jaundiced. You see what you're looking for. It doesn't take long for you to become impatient with your spouse's shortcomings and look for greener grass on the other side of the bed rather than staying home and fertilizing your own.

It's up to you to attract positive employees, vendors, and customers/clients; and select to do business with them.

Ask for Hope that Helps

It's also up to you to let go of any need you might have to do all the work yourself, thinking that it's easier for you to do it yourself than to involve others. When you conceive a work positive lifestyle, you accept help from others.

When our older daughter was two, like most two-year-olds, she was very intent on doing things for herself. "I do it, Daddy," she would tell me and then she would try and try to open the door, even though she could hardly reach the knob and the door weighed more than her. Or, she would try and try to make the puzzle piece fit upside down.

Sometimes, like all of us I guess, she wouldn't be able to do whatever she was attempting. But she would keep trying until she became so frustrated her words wouldn't come out right. In exasperation, she would say, "Hope me, Daddy," meaning to say, "Help me, Daddy."

Rather than take over for her and just do it myself, I replied, "OK, I'll help you." Then I would say something like, "Let's pull on the door together" or "Let's turn the puzzle piece another way and try it." And without fail, she and I together would do it.

As you learn to work positive, you'll probably try to do something that you think you can do on your own like our daughter. "I do it," you'll say. But then after trying to the point of frustration, you will realize that you could use the hope that help brings. That's when you transform your work lifestyle to a positive one by attracting positive team members.

Asking for hope that helps draws to you other hopeful people who are willing to help. Like the daylilies and birds, you receive what you require to make a work positive life in a negative world. All things in your life become possible as your team huddles around you, calling

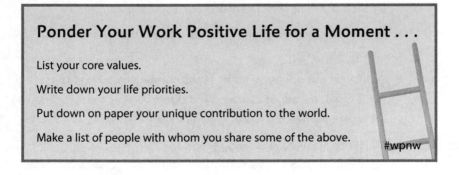

Ponder Your Work Positive Life for a Moment . . .

List your core values.

Write down your life priorities.

Put down on paper your unique contribution to the world.

Make a list of people with whom you share some of the above.

#wpnw

plays that the negative defenses of the world cannot stop. You gain much-needed information about gas furnaces, parachutes, frozen blue chunks, locked automobiles, autoconveyors, and anything else that used to be a knowledge deficit in your business. You discover customers and clients, employees and suppliers to lean on when business turns cold. You recall that you were fed, clothed, and cared for in ways that you fail to remember.

Tune yourself to attract those with whom you can redefine your reality, conceive how you will work positive, and make your dreams come true.

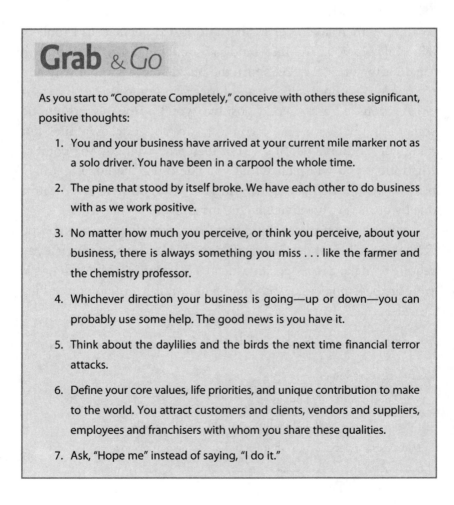

Grab & Go

As you start to "Cooperate Completely," conceive with others these significant, positive thoughts:

1. You and your business have arrived at your current mile marker not as a solo driver. You have been in a carpool the whole time.

2. The pine that stood by itself broke. We have each other to do business with as we work positive.

3. No matter how much you perceive, or think you perceive, about your business, there is always something you miss . . . like the farmer and the chemistry professor.

4. Whichever direction your business is going—up or down—you can probably use some help. The good news is you have it.

5. Think about the daylilies and the birds the next time financial terror attacks.

6. Define your core values, life priorities, and unique contribution to make to the world. You attract customers and clients, vendors and suppliers, employees and franchisers with whom you share these qualities.

7. Ask, "Hope me" instead of saying, "I do it."

CHAPTER 7

Compare and Compete Rarely

"It's hard to soar like an eagle when you're
flying with a bunch of turkeys."

—A bumper sticker

A duck hunter in town was said to have the best retriever in the county. But he refused to take anyone hunting with him to see the dog work. Finally, he agreed to let one friend go duck hunting with him. But he made the fellow promise not to tell anyone in town about his dog.

The friend promised, and so off they went duck hunting. He shot a duck, and the dog took off to retrieve the downed bird. But instead of swimming, the dog walked on the water to the downed bird, picked it up, and returned it, still walking on water, to the hunters.

The owner of the dog turned to his partner and said, "Now do you understand why I don't want you to tell anyone in town about my dog?"

"Yes, I do," the fellow replied. "I wouldn't want anybody to know I owned a dog that couldn't swim, either."

So how do you conceive your business—a dog that walks on water? Or a dog that can't swim?

Dogs that Didn't Swim

One of the largest challenges you and I face in conceiving the positive as we do business in the negative world is attracting positive people with whom to conceive. As we discovered in the previous chapter, our conceiving vibrations attract those who resonate with us—our core values, our life priorities, and our unique contributions we make to the world. Our businesses amplify these vibrations. If we vibrate negatively, those are the individuals we find ourselves partnering with. Such negative cooperation leads to what I call "negative conceiving."

For example, Ken Olsen, founder of Digital Equipment, in 1977 said something like, "There is no reason anyone would want a computer in their home." We have four computers in our home. How many do you have?

A Western Union Telegraph Company internal memo in 1876 read something like, "This 'telephone' has too many shortcomings to be seriously considered as a means of communication." Got a phone in your pocket or purse?

When Gary Cooper turned down the lead role in *Gone with the Wind*, he is reported to have said, "I'm just glad it'll be Clark Gable who's falling on his face and not Gary Cooper." Frankly, my dear, *Gone with the Wind* is a classic film and Gable is part of the reason it is.

In 1962 Decca Recording Company rejected the Beatles after a studio session, reportedly because "We don't like their sound, and guitar music is on the way out." How many Beatles songs can you name and sing?

"Negative conceiving" is everywhere. I have a friend who says that 95 percent of the time the people around you are wrong when they express their opinion. It's not that he thinks he is always right or that people do this intentionally. It's just the reality that unguided, most of us stumble down negative pathways and like Ken Olsen, Western Union, Gary Cooper, and Decca Records, miss the mark. We give away the power of our positive perceptions to people who negatively conceive with us. Unfortunately we listen to them too closely and follow their lead into dead-ends that keep us from a work positive lifestyle.

Think about it this way: what if Michael Dell chose to conceive with Ken Olsen? Or, what if Bell had taken to heart Western Union's analysis of his telephone? Or, what if Clark Gable had said, "Gary Cooper is right. I'm turning down this role." Or, what if John, Paul, George, and Ringo accepted at face value Decca Records' assessment, packed their guitars, and went back home to Liverpool? How would your world be different if any one of these scenarios became reality?

How Much Personal Power Do You Give to Drowning Dogs?

The reality of business is that all of us pursue negative pathways at times. We miss the mark just as these prominent persons and companies did. However, we have a choice about how much personal power we give away to others as we conceive our business worlds.

An airline pilot hammered his plane into the runway during a landing. His airline required him to stand in the door while the passengers exited, smile, and thank them for flying. He really didn't want to do this since his landing was anything but smooth.

Finally everyone had gotten off the plane except for this little old lady with a cane. The pilot breathed a sigh of relief until the lady asked him, "Sonny, mind if I ask a question?"

"Why no, ma'am," said the pilot. "What is it?"

She asked, "Did we land or were we shot down?"

Sometimes your best efforts at landing your business aren't successful. You get shot down and don't want to face others, particularly if your missed landing was very public. It is in these moments that you truly discover the kind of persons whom you have attracted into your business life. Positive people will encourage you to recover, remind you that mistakes are not fatal, and help you back up onto the work positive highway. Negative people will discourage you, ridicule you for even trying, and repel you down a negative cliff and drop you.

We all discover that we have attracted negative people into our lives at some point in the journey. Your imagination is calling to mind some of those very people right now.

Regardless of their actual names, I call them Eeyores. You remember Eeyore from Winnie the Pooh. Whenever Winnie the Pooh, Tigger, or Piglet would suggest some wonderfully positive pursuit, Eeyore's standard response was, "It'll never work."

We all find ourselves confronting Eeyores from time to time. The question for you becomes, "How much power will you give these Eeyores to conceive with you?" The real challenge for you as a business person is that the Eeyores you hire as employees or service as customers and clients or purchase from as vendors and suppliers aren't just cuddly cartoon characters from a children's book. In fact, they may be annoying as Eeyores by day, but actually they become vampires by night. They suck from you all the time, energy, and attention that you will allow them.

At night, they disturb your sleep with worry, which is nothing more than your imagination on negative steroids, and zap your energy for the next work day.

At night, they call your home and distract your attention away from your family who, though they may be the most patient people in the world, become exhausted by the intrusion.

At night, they take your time by . . . you fill in the blank here.

You know these Eeyore Vampires.

You wish they would just go away.

You know they won't.

So we're back to the question, "How much power will you give these Eeyore Vampires to conceive with you?"

What about your employee who expresses his opinion about you with regular negativity to his co-workers? How much time do you give to recovering your relationships with the other employees?

Or, what about the negative customer who throws a wet blanket on everything you try to do to please her with excellent customer service? How much energy do you waste on she-who-won't-be-pleased?

Or, what about the supplier who tells all the other competing vendors that you exclusively do business with him, preventing you from receiving the best bids? How much of your attention does he get?

Do You Compare and Compete?

The real challenge is when you allow Eeyore Vampires to have negative conceiving influence on you, you begin to compare and compete. When you compare and compete, you embrace a scarcity mindset of perception based on a negative view of reality that says, "There is not enough to go around in the universe. I got mine. You get yours." This negative view is antithetical to the true purpose of conceiving a work positive lifestyle which states that you are created to cooperate. By nature, cooperation suggests abundance; that working together we can achieve more than any one of us alone. To cooperate is to acknowledge that like the daylilies and birds, there is more than enough to go around for all of us.

When you compare and compete, inevitably you assume a superior-inferior relationship. Rather than embracing the creative diversity and its abundance endemic to the universe, you conceive with negativity that since I can accumulate more than you, I must be a better person than you. Inevitably you compare amounts of whatever you prize, and compete in an effort to prop up your fragile ego. You allow negative Eeyore Vampires the power to reverse the osmosis of your perceiving filter so that you filter out the positive and allow the negative to pass through.

Think about it this way. I have a favorite pair of blue jeans that I enjoy working in around the farm. I've snagged and ripped them on numerous occasions, so much so that some of the holes are pretty large. Let's say that I want to salvage these jeans because they're a favorite pair so I decide to patch them. If I choose to patch them with some of the finest silk from the best shop in Hong Kong, what would you think?

Or, let's say that my home is falling down. The foundation is crumbling on the north end. Therefore, my door jambs are tilting and the doors won't close. The floors are uneven and I trip on the hardwood boards sticking up. I decide to add on to my home and spend $200,000 building an addition off the sagging back porch. What would you think of my remodeling?

Or, imagine with me that instead of adding on to my falling down home, I decide to build a new home. I have a choice between building on a sandy stretch of beach, where a hurricane has come on shore three times in the last ten years, or at the base of a mountain on top of a granite slab that extends for miles underground. Which site should I choose?

Or, let's say that I'm blind and traveling to an unfamiliar city. I choose as my traveling companion a woman whom I met recently and who also happens to be blind. She has never been to this city either, but offers to act as my guide. Should I go with her?

Then why do you give away your power of choice to Eeyore Vampires who insist on a compare and compete style of conceiving business? Why do you allow them to form your company's reputation, your business's self-image, and your own self-perception of your work lifestyle?

It is the same as patching denim with silk, or adding on to a dilapidated dwelling, or building on weather-stricken sand, or letting the blind lead the blind.

A Better Way to Work

There is a better way to work than to compare and compete based on a scarcity conception driven by negativity.

Wayne Dyer told *Success* editor Darren Hardy a story about H.L. Mencken, who was a newspaper columnist. He wrote some columns that engendered a number of negative letters from his readers. In response, he wrote a column that basically said this: "I have your letters in hand that are critical of my recent columns. I am holding them in my hand while sitting in the smallest room in my home. Soon they will be behind me."

Rather than give away the power of influence over his self-esteem, self-image, and self-perception, Mencken chose a better way. He detached himself from the negativity and lived into his birthright of positive cooperation.

We spend so much energy and attention worrying about what others think about our business. We allow them to form our filters in negative ways. When we buy what they sell, we are complicit in this conspiracy by giving away our perception and conception of how we work positive. Is this the pathway to enjoying your work positive lifestyle?

The better way is to seek out teams of positive people. Like Mencken, deny the negative people your positive time, energy, and attention. Put them behind you. Avoid allowing them to take up space in your mind. Restrict their stealing minutes from your time like so many vampires. Their compare and compete version of work reality is not only unnecessary, it debilitates your enjoyment of the work positive lifestyle.

A coaching client came to our farm so he could spend some time away from the compare and compete world of his business and conceive with me the work positive lifestyle. It was the fall of the year and as we walked and talked down our driveway, we stopped beside a section of fence along a horse pasture. The sun was setting, casting its last rays of the day on the woods. Almost like a spotlight, the setting sun focused on a maple tree, its brilliant orange colors coming alive in the light until it appeared that it was on fire. It was quite a sight. My client noticed the tree, calling my attention to it.

Earlier in our walking, the conversation had turned to the compare and compete nature of life; of how critical others were of him and the professional barbs that became personal injuries he sustained by listening and taking to heart their negativity. As we stood there, leaning on the fence, soaking in the brilliance of the maple tree in the setting sun's rays, I noticed that the tree beside the maple was a cedar tree. Compared to the maple, the cedar was . . . well, "bland, nondescript, easily overlooked" all come to mind.

"Look at the cedar tree beside the maple," I said. "What do you see?"

"It doesn't look as good as the maple beside it," he said.

"But the cedar doesn't appear to be bothered by that, does it?" I asked. "In fact, it doesn't seem to care at all. It's just standing there, being a cedar tree, without any need to compare itself to the maple."

"It's just being a cedar and letting the maple be itself," he said. "I can do that."

When you compare and compete rarely, you give yourself permission to work positive as who you are, and you free others to do the same. As they pursue positivity in business, and you do the same, together you step away from the scarcity mentality of compare and compete and embrace your created nature of cooperation. Both of you are winners!

To compare and compete is to repair blue jeans with silk, add on an expensive dwelling to one falling down, build a home on a hurricane-ravaged beach, and ask a blind person to lead you as a blind person in an unfamiliar city. It is counterproductive to conceiving the positive at work with your employees and suppliers, customers and clients.

Compare and compete rarely.

As you do, you conceive the positive at work, avoiding the Eeyore Vampires and embracing the positive people you attract who choose to cooperate in your company's success. Once you live into your created purpose of cooperation and compare and compete rarely, then you are ready to conceive positivity at work on the ultimate level—by complementing with others.

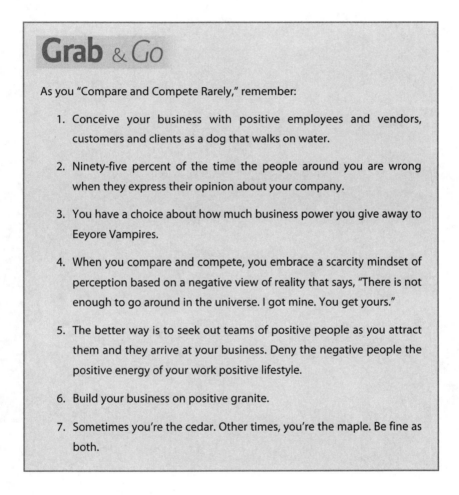

Grab & Go

As you "Compare and Compete Rarely," remember:

1. Conceive your business with positive employees and vendors, customers and clients as a dog that walks on water.

2. Ninety-five percent of the time the people around you are wrong when they express their opinion about your company.

3. You have a choice about how much business power you give away to Eeyore Vampires.

4. When you compare and compete, you embrace a scarcity mindset of perception based on a negative view of reality that says, "There is not enough to go around in the universe. I got mine. You get yours."

5. The better way is to seek out teams of positive people as you attract them and they arrive at your business. Deny the negative people the positive energy of your work positive lifestyle.

6. Build your business on positive granite.

7. Sometimes you're the cedar. Other times, you're the maple. Be fine as both.

CHAPTER 8

Complement with Others

"I believe that you should gravitate to people who are doing
productive and positive things with their lives."

—Nadia Comaneci

S omeone did an experiment with two groups of golfers. Each
group had a round of golf videotaped.

The video of the rounds was edited. The first group
was shown a video of their best shots—their longest drives, their
most accurate iron shots and chips, their one-putts. The instructor
conducting the experiment praised the golfers and told them to "go
out there and play like this again." So the golfers did. In fact, they
went out and actually improved their scores.

The second group was shown a video of their worst shots—
their drives that were topped, their shots that were hooked and
chips that went over the greens, their missed short putts. The
instructor conducting the experiment told these golfers, "People, is
this any way to play golf? Now go out there and fix those shots."
So the golfers immediately went out and played worse than before.

To which group of golfers would you prefer to belong?

The first group, of course.

But why?

The first group conceived their shots positively. Not only did their instructor cooperate with them to remind them of their most successful shots, but she complemented with them. Knowing that they would play better after viewing their best strokes, she cooperated by shooting video of those shots, and then took their play to the next level by encouraging them in their playing. The instructor and the golfers fit together successfully.

Conception Takes Two

This social dynamic of conceiving your work positive lifestyle in the negative world takes at least two. By nature, conception requires two persons contributing to the outcome. Basic biology, right? When conceiving in a complementary manner, at least two people contribute positively to an outcome that is more successful than either one of them could achieve alone. They positively work together for the mutual benefit of one another and others.

For example, we had just tucked our younger daughter in for a good night's sleep when a thunderstorm blew up. The wind whistled. The lightning flashed. The thunder rattled the windows. It was a pretty good-sized storm.

I heard all this sound-and-light show from downstairs in my recliner. Between the "booms" I heard this muffled voice calling, "Daddy! Daddy!" So I went upstairs to our younger daughter's bedroom where I found her with the covers pulled up over her head.

"What's wrong?" I asked.

"I'm scared of the thunder," she said. "Will you lie down with me?"

"Sure," I said as I got under the covers. "But why does it help with me under the covers?"

"Because the thunder can't hurt me when you're here. You're my Daddy," she said.

Doing business today gets pretty scary sometimes, doesn't it? Like when business is way off and you have an appointment with your banker to review your financials? Or your major supplier shortens his credit terms? Or your key employee goes to work for the competition down the street?

What do you do in those times?

Whom Do You Call?

Most likely you call the person who at some point in the past has conceived the positive in the negative world around you in a complementary way. She keeps your perspective on the long view, not the short term, when she's around. You are a better person when you are around him because he brings out the best in you and encourages you to do what you positively can do.

We bring out the best in one another when we share those common core values and life priorities of our work positive lifestyle, when we encourage one another's unique contribution to the world through our businesses. This ultimate level of conceiving how to work positive in the negative world occurs because you intentionally filter out the Eeyore Vampires and focus on cooperating with positive people who have abilities that are complementary to yours; different from yours yet which fit with yours like pieces of a puzzle. You avoid attracting to your business the ones who tell you, "It'll never work," and instead say, "Let's

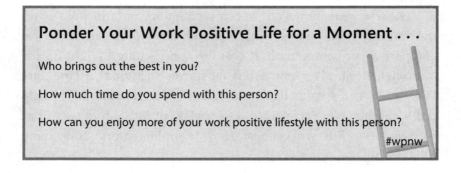

Ponder Your Work Positive Life for a Moment . . .

Who brings out the best in you?

How much time do you spend with this person?

How can you enjoy more of your work positive lifestyle with this person?

#wpnw

talk about how this will work positive." They show you your best, most successful business shots and encourage you to do it some more in the next quarter. That's work positive conceiving at the ultimate level—in a complementary way.

Who Brightens Your Day?

One fall, I planted some daffodils in front of one of my rose beds. They came up, bravely lifting their golden heads to see if winter really was gone and spring had come. They started timidly at first, just barely pushing up a green leaf or two. Then as they survived, more and more leaves emerged, until finally those golden heads shone through.

As they peeked and pushed up, I noticed something really interesting. Our home shades the daffodils from all the eastern, morning sun. Not a ray gets through, but the afternoon, western sun gets completely through, bathing the daffodils daily with its light and warmth.

As the daffodils' golden flowers popped through, guess which way they faced? That's right, every single one of them turned its cup towards the western sun.

Where does the warm light come from that nourishes your business?

Who are the people that brighten your office?

How can you enjoy more of your work life basking in time and experiences with them?

The daffodils enjoyed a complementary relationship with the sun. They cooperated with one another without any need for comparison or competition. It cost the sun nothing to light up the daffodils. It simply went about its normal activities as the sun. What good is the sun's light if not absorbed? The daffodils simply did what they were created to do—soaked up the sun rays.

See how life works best in a complementary conceiving relationship?

The same is true of your business and the people you attract to it.

It's Your Choice

You choose the people with whom you conceive your company in a complementary manner. You choose your customers and clients, employees and suppliers. One of the challenges is avoiding the isolationism that the compare-and-compete mental paradigm births in you and accepting that others really do want to help you achieve more at work than you ever have before. It is just a matter of becoming aware that you attract people to your business, looking around for who you're attracting, and inviting the ones who fit your work positive lifestyle to participate in a complementary conception of your business.

You already have everything you require to succeed in business.

A young son and his dad were walking through the woods one day. They approached a large rock and the little fellow said, "Hey Dad! Do you think I can lift that rock?"

"Of course you can," the dad said, "if you use all your strength."

The boy squatted down over the rock, put his hands around it, took a deep breath, and pulled on it as hard as he could. He failed to budge the rock even one inch.

Then he took an even deeper breath, and pulled on the rock even harder, grunting with all his might. Still the rock did not budge.

"I thought you said I could move this rock," the son said as he stood up next to his Dad.

"I did," the father replied, "but you didn't use all your strength."

The boy was indignant. "Yes, I did," he said. "I gave it all I had."

"But you didn't use all your strength," the dad insisted. "You could have asked me for help."

The compare-and-compete mentality of conceiving work paints us into a corner of existential angst with no viable exit. Alone, we make a mess every time. We sequester ourselves from others with whom we could enjoy a complementary relationship of work. We refuse to use all our strength which lies not only within ourselves, but within those close by who are ready to positively work with us to achieve that which we can only do with them. The impossible becomes possible when we enjoy a work positive lifestyle based on complementary conceiving relationships with others.

Our reality is redefined. We fulfill our dreams.

Knowing Them When You See Them

Perhaps you are wondering, "How do I recognize such persons with whose help I work positive?" There are five key characteristics to look for in people whom you attract. These are the people who want to enjoy a work positive lifestyle in which dreams come true despite the negative world.

Listen

The first characteristic is they listen.

Think about it this way: What if you went to see your medical doctor because you're sick? The nurse walks in, takes your temperature and blood pressure, asks you what's wrong, writes it down on your chart, and says, "The doctor will be in to see you in a moment."

And pretty soon the doctor walks in, reading your chart, and never looks up at you. He doesn't ask you what's wrong, where you hurt, how long you've been sick, "How 'bout those Patriots? Think they'll win another Super Bowl?" Nothing. He's just reading the chart.

All of a sudden he writes something down and says, "OK, I understand what's wrong with you. Here's a prescription. Pay at the window," and walks out.

Would you believe that doctor understands your condition?

No?

Why not?

The doctor did not listen to understand.

There is a line in the movie *Pulp Fiction,* that goes something like this: "Are you really listening, or just waiting to talk?"

Self-absorption is a symptom of a compare-and-compete lifestyle. Listening to another to the point of understanding is one of the hallmark qualities of someone with whom you want to work positive, a person who will conceive your business's best in the negative world in a complementary fashion. Such a person refuses any claim to know all the answers to your business questions without consultation. Instead they seek out mutually beneficial knowledge. They ask rather than assume.

My Grandfather Greene was just such a man. He was an entrepreneur—a crop farmer, dairy farmer, and proprietor of a country store—who understood the importance of leveraging complementary relationships in work positive ways. Once he bought a field on which to grow his crops. Of course before making the purchase, he learned everything he could about the field; analyzing the soil, determining the flow of water and its erosion, etc.

When he completed the purchase, another man who lived near the property approached my Grandfather as he worked the land. After exchanging their pleasantries, the man said to my Grandfather, "You know this is a hail field, don't you?"

"No," my Grandfather said. "What do you mean it's a hail field?"

"Well," the man said, "when the thunderstorms roll through here, and they do pretty often, the worst of the weather hits this field. I don't know why, but when we have hail over here, it's always on this field."

My Grandfather thanked the man for the information. The next day, he called his insurance agent and purchased twice the amount of insurance he normally secured a property and its crops with, based on the man's observation.

More often than not, the man was correct. If it hailed anywhere nearby, it hailed on that field, destroying the crops. My Grandfather was prepared. He covered his investment well, and often to his financial benefit, simply because he listened to the other man and understood. People with whom we can enjoy the work positive lifestyle in a complementary relationship listen to understand.

Ponder Your Work Positive Life for a Moment . . .

Remember an occasion in which you listened to understand someone and your business benefited from their knowledge and information. Call or write that person right now and express your gratitude.

#wpnw

Humility

A second key characteristic of these people with whom we team to work positive is humility. You know what humility smells like. Some people are not listening to you. They are waiting to talk. When you take a breath and they jump in, they talk mostly about themselves and most often their accomplishments. You wonder how they talk so much, deciding that they have gills instead of lungs and can talk without pausing to breathe. They smell like rotten egotism.

Others listen to you. They hang on your every word. They look you in the eye. They pause when you finish talking, absorbing your words and the tones and inflections behind them. They smell like sweet humility.

Humble people understand by their nature how complementary, work positive relationships work. Mutual benefit is a part of their vocabulary. When thrust into the limelight, they speak of others and their contribution to achieving the impossible. They redefine reality to include the team of people who fulfilled the dream.

We see such humility in NASCAR racing. Hundreds of thousands of fans crowd into luxury boxes and "chicken bone" seats just to watch their favorite drivers go as fast as they can around oval tracks, yelling and screaming at the top of their lungs, cheering them on. The drivers are the real celebrities here, making millions of dollars not just running cars, but endorsing everything from soft drinks to motor oil. The drivers make the headlines. It's the drivers who show up on a box of Wheaties. You can name at least one of these drivers, I bet . . . but can you name a tire changer? You see, while all this high-profile, big-money activity is going on, down in the pits is a team of guys who aren't asked to endorse anything. In fact, they'll never get their faces on anybody's box of cereal. But without this team of guys working together to change tires, fill gas tanks, make track bar adjustments, and clean windshields, the driver is dead on the track.

As it is with that driver, so it is with you and your business. You have a team of people helping your company go around daily. Those of us who are humble can name all these teams—employees and suppliers, customers and clients—who keep us going. In fact, we do name them, every opportunity we can. Humble people smell sweet because they use words like "we" and "us" and "the team."

Ponder Your Work Positive Life for a Moment . . .

. . . and name one team of people who keep your business on track.

Call or write them to say "thank you."

#wpnw

Mutual Benefit

A third key characteristic of those persons we attract and choose to complementary conceive the positive is they work with us for our mutual benefit. They share accomplishments with us, both the credit and the rewards. They genuinely don't care who gets the credit as long as the team benefits.

As I mentioned earlier, I really don't like squirrels because they steal the seed I buy for my birds. I read about and even bought a bird feeder called "The Absolute," a weight-sensitive device. The Century Tool & Manufacturing Co. of Cherry Valley, Illinois, made it with a counterweight device that shuts the feeder door when anything heavier than a bird lights on the feeder. When it first came on the market, Sue Wells, director of the National Bird-Feeding Society, says she and others thought someone "had finally come up with the ultimate solution."

But based on my personal observation along with others, squirrels have defeated this most ingenious device by teaming up with one another. While one squirrel stands on the counterweight bar behind the feeder, thereby keeping the front door from shutting, the other squirrel stands on the roost and feeds. Then they switch places.

These squirrels understand mutual benefit. If they can work positive for everyone's mutual benefit, maybe we can, too.

People with whom you want to conceive your work positive lifestyle choose mutual benefit for all involved. It is one of their

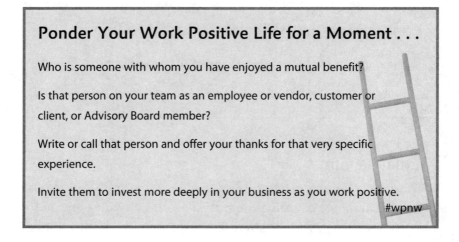

Ponder Your Work Positive Life for a Moment . . .

Who is someone with whom you have enjoyed a mutual benefit?

Is that person on your team as an employee or vendor, customer or client, or Advisory Board member?

Write or call that person and offer your thanks for that very specific experience.

Invite them to invest more deeply in your business as you work positive.

#wpnw

core values and life priorities. It drives the unique contribution they offer to the world as they work positive.

These are the people you want to attract, choose, and invite onto the work positive team of your business.

Accountability

A fourth characteristic of people who desire to work positive with you in the negative world in a complementary way is they hold us accountable. They bring out the best in us by asking questions that force us to be surgically honest with ourselves. Such questions are not intended to embarrass or humiliate us. Instead they create a healthy amount of pressure that forces us into those habits and patterns that shape our business into its preferred level of success.

Let's say that you have a rubber band in your hand. It lays there in a certain shape. You pick up the rubber band and stretch it out and around a stack of cards. The band has changed its shape in response to the stack of cards and the pressure you put on it to fit. As long as it is around the cards, the band maintains that shape. Relieve the pressure by taking it off the cards and what happens? It goes back to its original shape.

Your business is like that rubber band. It requires accountability to be built into your complementary conceiving relationships. One of the reasons we are at our best with another person is the give-and-take of such relationships, the encouragement to do and be better; the reality that this person with whom we conceive depends on and benefits from our best efforts. It is this very pressure that keeps us in tip-top shape, focusing on the work positive lifestyle and filtering out the negative. Just as long as we are in this relationship, we enjoy a work positive shape of guiding our business behavior with our core values, of living out of our life priorities, and of making our unique contribution. Remove the pressure of the relationship, we start goose-stepping our way back into the negative line of people

Ponder Your Work Positive Life for a Moment . . .

. . . and consider, "Who is the person who puts healthy pressure on me to be at my best at work?"

How can you best express your appreciation to this person?

#wpnw

who populate the world and run their businesses in a compare-and-compete manner.

The Golden Rule

The fifth and final characteristic we can recognize in complementary conceiving people with whom we work positive is that they live out of the Golden Rule. They do unto others as they wish for others to do unto them. They treat others the way they want to be treated. They are humble listeners who work for our mutual benefit and keep us accountable. In fact, the Golden Rule is the foundation of our conceiving relationships.

By now, you definitely have thought of numerous people with whom you enjoy such a Golden Rule, work positive relationship. However, you probably have thought of some folks who possess anything but these characteristics. (See how familiar that negative neural pathway is?) You might have even spent a few minutes wondering why they are the way they are. Never mind the reality we discussed earlier that something resonating within you attracts them, right?

Perhaps you think of them as not just negative persons, Eeyore Vampires, but as your enemies. Remember—what you resist, persists. So simply telling yourself, "I shouldn't be thinking about these enemies" causes your mind to focus on them even more. You may even relive painful experiences with them.

Rather than castigating yourself for recalling these folks as enemies of your business success, and instead of resisting these thoughts and causing yourself to persist in them, look at your enemies differently. What if we are grateful for our enemies? Now I know that sounds very counterintuitive, causing everything in you to rebel, but think about it for a minute. What if, instead of demonizing them, you interpret your experiences with them as opportunities to bring out the best in you?

How? Reality suggests we tend to dislike in others what we dislike about ourselves. So if one of your enemies has a certain core value or life priority that really bothers you, consider why that is. Could it be that you see your own core value or life priority and the way you live it out in your business reflected back? Or that you struggle with the temptation to work that way and don't like that about yourself?

Redefine your reality about your enemies so you can fulfill your dreams. Sure, you will most likely never choose to be in a work positive, complementary relationship with this Eeyore Vampire; he reflects back to you negativity from the world. But what have you really done if you return negativity for negativity? Simply multiplied the Gross Negative Product around you, right? Thus sending out more negative vibrations that attracts more negative people as customers and clients, vendors and employees who you classify as enemies . . . and the cycle perpetuates.

Instead, see this person's negative behavior as the opposite of what you are all about. Use it to keep yourself accountable. Let it bring out the best in you which is your ultimate business investment, making you more intentional about working positive through complementary relationships.

Look back and ask yourself, "Who are the people who invested in me, my business, and our well-being? Who gave of themselves with a reasonable expectation of return?"

Thank them. Celebrate them.

Look around now and ask yourself, "Who are the people currently investing in me, my business, and our well-being? Who is giving of themselves with a reasonable expectation of return?"

Thank them. Celebrate them.

Now look forward and ask, "Who are the people I choose to invest in with a reasonable expectation of return? How do I move toward them to coach them to work positive like I do?"

As you look back, around you, and ahead, you build your Work Positive Team of conceiving, complementing people in the midst of this negative world. They are humble listeners who work for the mutual benefit of all and keep one another accountable in golden ways.

These people conceive a work positive lifestyle even in the negative world around them . . . and so do you.

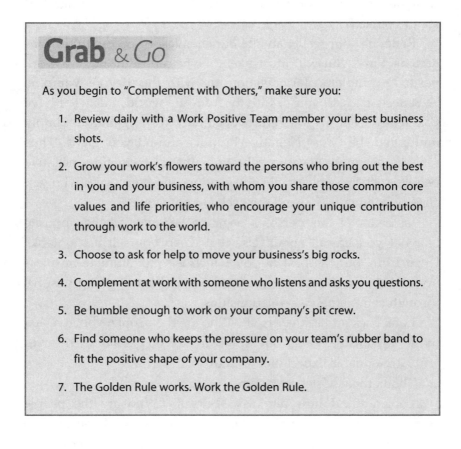

Grab & Go

As you begin to "Complement with Others," make sure you:

1. Review daily with a Work Positive Team member your best business shots.

2. Grow your work's flowers toward the persons who bring out the best in you and your business, with whom you share those common core values and life priorities, who encourage your unique contribution through work to the world.

3. Choose to ask for help to move your business's big rocks.

4. Complement at work with someone who listens and asks you questions.

5. Be humble enough to work on your company's pit crew.

6. Find someone who keeps the pressure on your team's rubber band to fit the positive shape of your company.

7. The Golden Rule works. Work the Golden Rule.

"I BELIEVE in the POSITIVE at Work"

CHAPTER 9

"I Believe"

"I have learned that if one advances confidently in the direction of his dreams, and endeavors to live the life he has imagined, he will meet with a success unexpected in common hours."

—Henry David Thoreau

I t was one of those snows you remember for a long time, at least when you live in a part of the world that rarely gets snow, like the beach. It was a large enough snow to make a huge snowman. My wife, older daughter who was almost 3 years old, and I did just that—rolling and piling snow into this 6-foot snowperson. We gave our creation ginger snap eyes, a carrot nose, stick arms, and chocolate chip cookie buttons. My daughter insisted we put a hat on him. And, of course, we named him Frosty.

You see, while we watched the snow fall I read her the story of Frosty and how he came to life one day. So we had to name him Frosty.

After we finished our Frosty, we stood back and admired him. As we did, she asked, "Daddy, when is he gonna come alive?" She remembered the story.

"I don't know, honey. We'll have to watch and wait," I said.

How do you tell your daughter who believes in the magic of an old silk hat that it's not real? That the story is just a fairy tale written to entertain children?

The next day brought the same question: "Daddy, when is he gonna come alive?"

"I don't know, honey. We'll have to watch and wait," I said. I knew my answer would not satisfy her the next day, but what else could I say?

When the next day came, it brought the same question as before, "Daddy, when is he gonna come alive?"

All I could think of was a miserable, "I don't know, honey."

But she was ready with an answer even if I wasn't.

"I know, Daddy," she said. "He comes alive when we're not looking."

There is more to business than we think there is, because what we think exists is based primarily on our perception of reality. Or, it is based on our experiences with others. As good as our conception is, particularly when we complement with positive people, there is still a *je ne sais quoi* that redefines our understanding of reality. There is much to business that comes alive when we are not looking.

You hold certain beliefs about your company—its employees, its customers and clients, its profit margin, its gross revenue, its ability to financially provide for you and your family to enjoy more discretionary time. You emotionally invest your beliefs in your business based on your experiences with it. As accurate as your beliefs based in relationships and experiences might be, there is still much about your business that redefines reality. Your company, with all of its varied expressions, comes alive from time to time when you're not looking.

But for this redefinition of reality, this realm of business operations that exists beyond our constant awareness and defies description in Quickbooks, we would find it impossible to work positive in a negative world. Why? Because what we think about and experience with others would be all there is. Unfortunately that is negative for many people much of the time. You've been there, done that, and collected all the logoed shirts, right?

The wonderful aspect of this other realm of your business is that you can become aware of it, and even work into it. In fact, you came into this world to make this unique contribution through your company knowing that there's more to life than you can perceive and conceive. Remember being fed at two o'clock in the morning?

To work positive, you perceive and conceive the positive in a negative world, and you also believe your business can come alive when you're not looking; that there are resources beyond your immediate control that converge in miraculous ways.

Knowing how to perceive your work positive lifestyle in this negative world, focusing on the positive while avoiding just the "familiar," and then placing the positive filter on your thoughts is the first step to work positive. The second step is to conceive your work positive lifestyle by cooperating with and surrounding yourself with positive people who complement what you perceive instead of comparing and competing. The third step, "I Believe," is to redefine your notion of reality and believe that your business can positively exceed even your expectations, despite this negative world. This step is the emotional dynamic of how you work positive.

CHAPTER 10

Believe Your Birthright

You'll see it when you believe it.

—Wayne Dyer

Did you hear about the man who took his first airplane ride? He didn't really want to go, but was finally persuaded to try it. Scared to death, he got in the plane. The pilot took off, circled the field and landed safely. Someone asked him, "Well, now that wasn't so bad, was it?"

And the man said, "I'll tell you this much. I never did put my full weight down in that thing!"

Do You Trust the Unfamiliar?

I can relate with that guy. Many times I don't trust something new. There are other times when I'm just afraid of stepping out and trying it.

Why? Because my perception and conception of my companies in which I'm trying to work positive are limited to my five senses, only the things I can see and hear, taste and touch and smell. The real challenge for this definition of reality is that my senses are not always accurate. There is a realm of reality beyond my own senses.

Take for instance when you're forecasting sales and revenue. If you work positive in a retail environment, you analyze a great deal of data like traffic counts and patterns, demographic information within a certain geographic proximity to your location, and psychographic profiles of your ideal customer. Then you determine a percentage of these figures, based on other research you did regarding industry standards, projecting how many customers will spend what amount of money within a certain time frame. In doing so, you create a year one, two, and three sales forecast. Based on the best information you can find, you believe your retail operation will do this amount of business.

As you work positive through year one, two, and three, a different reality emerges. In some quarters, your business comes alive when you're not looking. You exceed your forecast. In other quarters, you come close, but not exactly hit your marks.

There is a realm of reality beyond your senses.

For instance, a couple of sisters walk into a Goodwill store in Danville, Virginia. They are mostly browsing, just slightly interested in anything particular, and more interested in the shopping. One sister finds an attractive pearl necklace. She likes it, tries it on, and decides to buy it for 69 cents.

She returns home to Arizona where she wears the pearls and someone compliments her. She tells her story to which the person responds, "Oh, I think they're worth more than 69 cents. You should have those appraised."

She did. The pearl necklace was valued at $50,000. A little more than the purchase price of 69 cents.

Our definition of reality misses the target sometimes. We put our full weight down without even knowing it, don't we?

Do you think the donor of that necklace to Goodwill would like that one back? Or, that Goodwill wishes it knew then what it knows now? Reality gets redefined quickly. Resources beyond our ability to influence, control, or manipulate converge in unexplainable ways.

Here's another example. A man was walking through a gem and mineral show when he saw a potato-sized rock. It was not attractive at all, rather garish, in fact, particularly when compared to all the other beautiful stones. The price tag read $20.

"You want $20 for this?" the man asked the vendor.

The vendor said, "Well, yeah, but you can have it for $10."

The $10 potato-sized rock turned out to be a star sapphire weighing more than 1,000 carats and worth more than $1 million.

Again, our definition of reality misses the target. We put our full weight down without even knowing it.

Do you think the vendor of that "rock" wanted a "do-over" on that one? Reality gets redefined quickly.

We define reality based on our best information and interpretation of our experiences. This reality is rooted in an outward appearance, those factors evident to us. In fact, there is a reality beyond the apparent.

My grandmother gave my brother and me a chocolate bunny every spring when I was a kid. I always looked forward to getting it, but there were some chocolate bunnies I liked better than others. I never really knew which chocolate bunny I had received until I bit into it because they all looked alike.

Some years when I bit into the bunny, there was nothing but air inside. She gave us a hollow chocolate bunny.

Other years, I bit into the chocolate bunny which looked like the hollow bunnies and discovered that she gave us a marshmallow-filled one. It was great because at least it had something inside.

My favorite years were those when I bit into the chocolate bunny that looked exactly like the hollow and marshmallow-filled ones and found that our grandmother gave us a solid chocolate bunny. They were chocolate all the way through.

We never knew which kind of bunny we had until we bit into it. Reality gets redefined bite by bite. What appears to be apparent changes.

You Are Born to Believe

Suffice it to say then that our version of business reality misses the target sometimes. There is much to the businesses we run as we work positive that we simply misunderstand. There is much more to employee relations, customer satisfaction, and vendor contracts than we can see and hear, taste, touch, and smell.

We are born to believe that reality defies our description and experience. Like my older daughter and her Frosty the Snowman, you have had many similar experiences in which your business came alive when you were not looking. Resources converged in miraculous ways that you just didn't anticipate.

I speak to and coach a lot of insurance agents in how to work positive in a negative world. When I talk with them about this third step—believe—I ask them to remember an occasion when they made a presentation to a prospective client that seemed to go nowhere. They could find no positive traction or reaction at all from the client. Perhaps the response was, "I want to think about it." They left the appointment saying, "Well, I'll never hear from that person again."

A few days, or weeks, or months later, the agent gets a call from that same client saying something like, "I know you recommended I buy $250,000 of term life insurance, but I think I want to go with the $1,000,000 universal policy instead. Is that OK with you?" Of course, the agent says "Yes!" and once again experiences how quickly reality redefines for us when unexpected resources converge.

Our version of reality is less than ultimate. Remember the daylilies and birds and how they inexplicably point to a universal abundance? Out of that same abundance, resources converge that are beyond our ability to control much less manipulate and even at times influence.

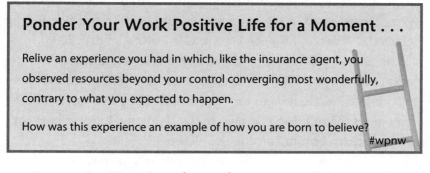

Ponder Your Work Positive Life for a Moment . . .

Relive an experience you had in which, like the insurance agent, you observed resources beyond your control converging most wonderfully, contrary to what you expected to happen.

How was this experience an example of how you are born to believe?

#wpnw

You read earlier about how when I was a little boy, I loved playing baseball. I played third base for the Little League White Sox team. Brooks Robinson was my third-base idol. My plans were for him to play for the Orioles until I grew up and came to take his place at the "hot box."

Also, I batted fourth in our lineup, the "cleanup" position. Henry Aaron was my hero. He made the ball fly out of any park on any given day. I dreamed of meeting him one day.

I still remember one great game I had at the plate with several base hits, driving in some runs. I came to bat with two outs, runners on base. Visions of "Hammerin' Hank" ran through my mind.

The other team changed pitchers, putting in their best one—a big guy with a fastball that sizzled as it popped into the catcher's mitt.

I stepped into the batter's box, ready to get a base hit. But after three pitches, the umpire screamed, "Strike 3, you're out!"

I couldn't believe it. I had struck out.

I remember walking back to the dugout, my eyes filling with tears of disappointment. My coach, Ed Shackleford, met me halfway with the words, "It's all right, Joey. You'll get 'em next time."

In that moment of utter childhood disappointment, I refused to believe there would be a "next time." I believed that this particular at-bat was it. My coach redefined my reality. He believed that there would be a next time. I could not see beyond my failure in the moment. He believed that not only would there be a next time, but that I would get a hit. I didn't think I would ever hit the ball again. He believed in me and that I would be all right. Because he believed, I did, too. I finished the season batting above .500.

Since our minds crave the familiar, having already created neural pathways with folders ready to receive similar information, believing is a challenge for we mature, sophisticated adults. Remember the old dog and new tricks? How the hardest part isn't the new tricks, but unlearning the old ones?

As children, we are still carving out neural pathways. From the moment of our birth, we imprint people and experiences with a certain sense of awe and wonder over the many faces of reality. New experiences thrill us because we are fascinated with life. We are like sponges absorbing everything.

That's why to believe that you can work positive in this negative world, you must reclaim your birthright to believe. You were born to believe. Hourly as a child you lived in and believed the reality that life is much more about what you misunderstand than it is about what you do. It is only as an adult you began to define your reality as what you can influence, control, and manipulate. Those same mental folders labeled "Familiar" shaped and formed your version of reality. You believe only in what you know to be true.

Your version of reality determines to a great extent how well your business performs. The way you believe your company succeeds, combined with how you perceive and conceive it, charts the course into red or black ink.

Fortunately, the reality of how we work positive is far more vast than what we know. Our perceptions are limited. Our conceptions are limited. We willingly suspend our disbelief to at least acknowledge that the borders of our version of reality are pretty close in. Whether we realize it or not, we put our full weight down in this larger-than-life reality. Our understanding of reality devalues based on appearance those things worth much, much more like inexpensive necklaces and potato-sized rocks. Experiences we thought dead-ended come back to life with a picture of reality we never dreamed possible. There is far more to your work positive lifestyle than you ever imagine.

As children, we understand that there is an ultimate reality that we cannot see but only glimpse, that we cannot hear except in a whisper, that we cannot taste but only sip, that we cannot touch but just feather-brush lightly, that we cannot smell but only catch a faint whiff. We believe in this ultimate reality, even if it only comes alive when we are not there. Because we believe, we grow towards what our open sense of honest inquiry reveals to us. We trust what we are born to believe in and grow in that direction.

How Does Your Belief in Your Business Grow?

I was working out on our farm one beautiful afternoon, clearing small trees and brush away from our electric fence line. I worked along a section of fence and noticed something really interesting.

There were three saplings growing together. The farthest sapling was under the shade of a more mature tree so it received less light. Here's the interesting part: that sapling, instead of growing straight up in search of light in the mature tree's shade, changed its growth pattern. The sapling grew at a 45-degree angle up through its companion saplings. It grew toward the light, changing its normal way of growing. In fact, it not only grew at a 45-degree angle through the other saplings toward the light, it had grown taller and fuller than the others.

How interesting is that? The sapling grew into the light, doing what it was born to do. Yet you and I who were born to believe grow away from that light, choosing instead to believe only in what we can see and hear, taste and touch and smell.

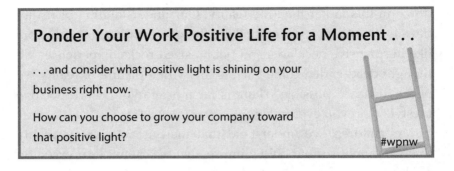

Ponder Your Work Positive Life for a Moment . . .

. . . and consider what positive light is shining on your
business right now.

How can you choose to grow your company toward
that positive light?

#wpnw

We Rarely Pull the Load Alone

When we deny our birthright to believe, we try to do something
apart and alone from the converging of resources in unexplainable
ways and discover that we can't. We bear the weight of doing
business alone, taking on so many responsibilities that we redefine
ourselves from "human being" to "human doing." Persistent as we
are, we nonetheless push on the problem with an employee, or kick
the chaos of credit extensions, or deny the dilemma of a dissatisfied
customer, and no matter what we do, we just can't budge it. We
can't pull the load alone so we just sit down and quit, refusing to
believe, to engage ourselves emotionally in new, broader solutions
that lie just outside our version of reality.

The story is told of a man driving a wagon pulled by a mule
named Jim. When everyone got on the wagon, the driver yelled,
"Giddyup, Jim. Giddyup, Sue. Giddyup, Sam. Giddyup, John.
Giddyup, Joe."

As the wagon started to move, one of the passengers was rather
mystified by the wagon master calling all those names. He said,
"When Jim is the one and only mule you have there, why do you
call the other names?"

And the owner said, "If Jim knew he was the only one pulling
this wagon, he'd never budge an inch."

We really don't know what our companies can do until we claim
our birthright to believe that we are yoked with a team of infinite

resources that pull along with us, creating our positive success. Our perception and conception can create a lot more horsepower for dealing with our business challenges than we imagine . . . until we believe, until we emotionally engage our businesses at a level of success that we've previously left unexplored. When we do, the impossible becomes possible.

We were born to believe in the ultimate reality of the work positive lifestyle that is far more vast than what we know. Our perceptions are limited. Our conceptions are finite. We willingly suspend our disbelief in order to at least acknowledge that the artificial borders of reality we place around our businesses are pretty close in. Whether we realize it or not, we put our full weight down in this larger-than-life reality. Our understanding of the reality of doing business the way everyone else does devalues those things worth much, much more like pearl necklaces and potato-sized rocks. Experiences we gave up on resurrect with a reality that defies description.

"How did that happen?" we ask.

There is far more to the work positive lifestyle than we ever imagine.

You were born to believe that there is more capacity in your business and its ability to produce the kind of lifestyle you want for yourself and your family than you've previously imagined. Every day you must claim this birthright if you want to work positive, because the negative world seeks to deny you of your birthright.

When you turn away from your birthright to believe—and we all do—you bend away from the positive light of unlimited, converging resources and toward your own ego. Such a bend severely limits the growth of your business and distorts your lifestyle toward a work-negative one.

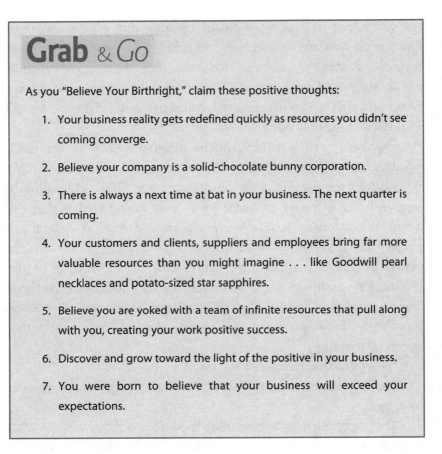

Grab & Go

As you "Believe Your Birthright," claim these positive thoughts:

1. Your business reality gets redefined quickly as resources you didn't see coming converge.

2. Believe your company is a solid-chocolate bunny corporation.

3. There is always a next time at bat in your business. The next quarter is coming.

4. Your customers and clients, suppliers and employees bring far more valuable resources than you might imagine . . . like Goodwill pearl necklaces and potato-sized star sapphires.

5. Believe you are yoked with a team of infinite resources that pull along with you, creating your work positive success.

6. Discover and grow toward the light of the positive in your business.

7. You were born to believe that your business will exceed your expectations.

CHAPTER 11

Bend Away from Ego

*"Success is never final; failure is never fatal.
It's courage that counts."*

—Winston Churchill

I t seems as if all I'm hearing these days is bad news, mostly centered around the world economy. I'm observing a lot of people becoming so frightened that they're not trying. They are afraid of failing.

Does It Feel Like the First Time?

Are you one of these people? Well, if you are, there's nothing to be afraid of. You've failed before, and lived to succeed another day.

While you probably don't remember it, you failed the first time you tried to walk. That's right, you fell down. Thankfully, you wore a diaper to buffer your bottom. You got up and kept trying until you stayed up on your wobbly legs. You're walking today, right? You chose to get up when you fell.

And I'll bet you almost drowned the first time you tried to swim, didn't you? But you stayed in the water until you learned to trust it to support you. Today you swim, right?

Did you hit or kick a ball the first time you swung at it? You may have fallen flat on your backside, but you stayed after it until you made contact. You can hit or kick a ball today, right?

What about riding a bike? Remember skinning your knees and elbows, crying while your parent cleaned you up? Yet you can ride a bike today, right?

It takes a great deal of courage to keep trying in the face of failure. Our natural human response is to give up, to find something we're good at; to do only those activities in which we have demonstrated our prowess rather than risk humiliation and embarrassment . . . again; to influence, control, and manipulate those things and people around us to conform to our standards of behavior or thinking or believing—our perfect reality, perfect because we're in charge.

In short, rather than believing in our birthright that we can work positive and our businesses come alive when we are not looking, or willingly suspending our disbelief in the face of the negative economic reality screaming all around us, or at least acknowledging that resources converge at times in ways we did not accomplish, we choose to exercise our egos.

Warning Sign: Dead-End Ahead

Such exertion is the pathway to the dead-end of our assumed perfection. It is assumed perfection because our egotistical logic runs something like this:

"If I can just influence, control, and manipulate my customers and clients, vendors and employees, along with my books, I will be successful. My business will run according to my schedule. I will accomplish my goals in my time. I will have everything I want. I

Ponder Your Work Positive Life for a Moment . . .

What or who are you trying to influence, control, and manipulate?

So, how's this logic working for you?

#wpnw

will work harder, be more brilliant than my peers, and do more than anybody else. My business lifestyle will be perfect."

The self-made businessman or woman lives negatively, restricted by the limitations of his or her ego-driven choices, pursuing an assumed perfection that exists only as a fantasy masquerading as reality, that is only a façade propped up by this negative world.

Avoid such self-made Eeyore Vampires as if they have a deadly, communicable disease.

Because they do.

Unfortunately we can't always avoid them.

Because sometimes we are them.

Have You Met Yourself Lately?

That's right. Sometimes we allow the negative noise of business to crowd out the positive song we long to hear. We stop up our ears, hum to ourselves, and believe the lie.

One cold winter's night, I was sitting in my favorite recliner at home, trying to have a conversation with my wife. She was seated in the chair next to me with only a lamp table between us.

Suddenly I realized that I was yelling to be heard. So I listened around the room for a moment and discovered why. First, the TV was on, blaring through our speaker system. It had to be on loud enough to be heard over the fan that was blowing hot air from the gas logs. Because the gas logs were on and dry out the air, we were running a humidifier with its fan blowing. Throw in a couple of daughters talking, and it's no wonder I was yelling.

So I got up out of my recliner and turned off the humidifier, turned back the fan blowing hot air from the gas logs, turned down the TV, and said, "Shhh" to our daughters. Then I sat back down, smiled at my wife, and said, "There, that's better."

Does the noise of your business prevent you from hearing success? It is so easy to disbelieve that the universe exists to support us, intersecting the very means required for our accomplishing the impossible in our businesses. As we disbelieve this ultimate reality, we bend our corporations into ourselves, specifically our egos and the assumed perfection we fantasize about. Our business becomes about what we can do and did once upon a time. I refer to it as economic navel gazing. We become self-consuming. The insatiable emotional appetite of our egos black-hole everything positive, spewing only narrow, negative noises. These noises interfere with our creating a work positive lifestyle. They become:

Fears about finances—"The bank called. Surely they're not calling in my note because of a down month."

Suspicions about an employee—"He sure talks about our competition a lot. Could he be feeding them information?"

Mistrust of a vendor—"She says she's doing me a special favor with this contract and I have known her for 10 years, but I wonder if she's telling the truth."

The circular list goes on and on.

These noisy worries assault our ability to work positive. They cause us to bend further toward our egos in pursuit of our assumed perfection, or at least the skill to pull ourselves up by our own bootstraps.

Business Will Be Better When . . .

So here you are sitting in your office, staring at a profit and loss or bank statement, negative noise booming through your ego. You begin talking to yourself and the conversation starts with, "I'll be OK. Business will be better when . . .

> I get some new employees."
> I move to a new location."
> I renegotiate my supplier contracts."
> I cut out my distributor and sell direct."
> I . . . I . . . I . . . ."

Sure, you're important to your business. You may be your business.

However, you are not the sum total of your business.

It just seems that way when the economic noise assaults you at incredibly difficult decibel levels and your first recourse is to bend in to your ego. You then set up unrealistic "perfect stages" of your business' life when everything will be just right.

Your ego fears failure, rejection, and a host of other paralyzing scenarios, none of which exist except in your emotions. This fear prevents you from getting up and doing what you can do, controlling what you can control, and avoiding worrying about the rest.

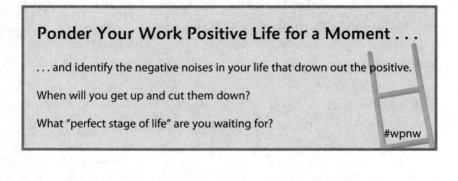

Ponder Your Work Positive Life for a Moment . . .

. . . and identify the negative noises in your life that drown out the positive.

When will you get up and cut them down?

What "perfect stage of life" are you waiting for?

#wpnw

It's a Sweet and Sour Life

The reality is from the moment you filed papers to incorporate, or even before that—when your business was an idea you had while driving down the highway—from that moment until now you have experienced challenges. What you believe about these challenges determines your business reality and whether you fulfill your dreams.

Are these challenges the worst of times?

Or, are they the best of times?

Some years ago when both our daughters lived at home, my wife prepared sweet and sour chicken for supper. I watched as our older daughter ate her third piece. I said to her, "You really like sweet and sour chicken, don't you?"

"Yes, sir!" she said. "But I like the sweet part best. I told Mama I just wanted the sweet, not the sour part of the sauce."

Then my wife said, "But I explained to her that the sweet and the sour were together in the sauce and that I couldn't separate them."

"That's OK," our daughter said as she ate that third piece, "I still like the sweet part best."

I'm like our daughter. I like just the sweet part of owning a business. No sour experiences for me! Nothing like an unexplained drop in sales to make my tongue curl or my mouth pucker up. No key employee leaving to start his own business to cause my eyes to water. No unanticipated increase in fuel costs that drives up shipping charges to churn my stomach acid.

I want everything to go my way. That's the assumed perfect business for me!

But as much as I like the sweet part best just as my daughter did, my wife is right. As it is with sauce, so it is with doing business. It's just the way running a company is: the sweet and the sour are together.

The way you do business best is more about what you believe to be reality than you ever imagined. Maybe that's why you picked up this book about how to *Work Positive in a Negative World*. You know the sour parts, the negativity of owning a business. You have exercised your ego to the point of exhaustion, trying to make something perfect out of your problems, or to at least get some forward momentum. You're hoping there is more left in your company, more than what you and your ego have done so far.

The good news for us all is that there is much, much more to owning a business than what we have done so far. Remember that moment when your business was just an idea? Hope for that idea succeeding peeks up through the cold adversity of your ego-constructed, assumed-perfection company like the first crocus of spring through six inches of snow.

You were born to believe that you can work positive and generate success, avoiding bending inward to your ego. That's something you do to yourself when you allow the negative world to take over your emotions.

You are actually at your best, enjoying a work positive lifestyle, when you live into your birthright to believe and imagine how you can best work positive in a negative world. Let's discover how.

Grab & Go

As you work to "Bend Away from Ego," remember:

1. When you were first learning to walk, you fell down more than you walked. Yet you walk today. Keep believing.

2. Avoid self-made Eeyore Vampires as if they have a deadly, communicable disease. Because they do. Unfortunately we can't always avoid them. Sometimes we are them.

3. Noisy worries assault your desire to work positive.

4. Your business life is always filled with challenges. Choose to build on the sweet parts while acknowledging the sour.

5. You were born to believe, not to bend inward to your ego.

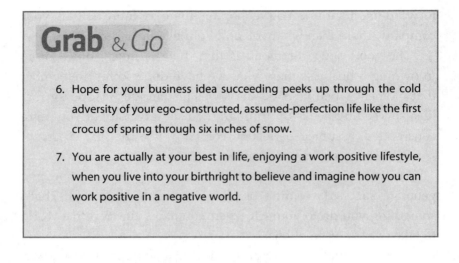

Grab & Go

6. Hope for your business idea succeeding peeks up through the cold adversity of your ego-constructed, assumed-perfection life like the first crocus of spring through six inches of snow.

7. You are actually at your best in life, enjoying a work positive lifestyle, when you live into your birthright to believe and imagine how you can work positive in a negative world.

CHAPTER 12

Best to Imagine

"We have a positive vision of the future founded on the belief that the gap between the promise and reality of America can one day be finally closed. We believe that."

—Barbara Jordan

A friend of mine traveled through Ireland with a tour group. They drove by bus through the beautiful countryside, admiring the rolling hills and green pastures.

My friend noticed that trees bordered the road. The more she looked at them the more she realized that they were all planted and grown the exact distance apart. She asked her tour guide about the trees.

"Oh, yes," the tour guide told her. "Those trees were originally fence posts cut locally from trees. They were planted exactly five feet apart as fence posts. The soil is so rich here that the planted fence posts started sprouting limbs and eventually grew into trees again."

> ## Ponder Your Work Positive Life for a Moment . . .
>
> . . . and honestly answer this question: Would you have imagined
> that fence posts can grow into trees again? Why?
>
> #wpnw

Are You Settling for Less Than?

When you bend your business to your ego, you forfeit your created capacity to believe, and define your company's practices as only those things and people that you can influence, control, and manipulate. With this corporate policy of assumed perfection, you give away the keys to your ability to imagine your business as wildly successful.

As we discovered in the first step of "I Perceive," your mind is content without imagining. Since your mind abhors the unfamiliar, preferring instead to more efficiently file away the Familiar in previously established categories, you are mentally by nature satisfied. It is OK with your mind not to imagine your company as achieving anything more than it is right now.

However, doing business today confronts you, at times even assails you, with the unfamiliar. The context in which you transact business changes every single day you open the doors and answer the phone. If you play to your mind's laziness and refuse to accept these unfamiliar perceptions, by default you bend to your ego. You stand in your business's batting cage and refuse to swing at anything thrown at you except those few pitches you recognize. In your assumed perfection, you settle for less than you can achieve by redefining your reality. You stop short of fulfilling your dreams. And if you keep your business alive long enough, you reach a point at which you say, "I wish I had known so I could have done something about it."

Our younger daughter had an experience like this. She really doesn't like to get up in front of a crowd. She is introverted and prefers small groups to large crowds. It was a big deal for her when she sang in the elementary school chorus at a Parents-Teachers Organization (PTO) meeting of several hundred people.

Of course she did great, knowing all the lyrics and following her director closely. Afterwards, as we drove home and talked, she was so relieved that the whole thing was over.

"How did you feel?" I asked her.

"My stomach felt funny when I was up on the stage," she said.

I told her, "Oh, those were butterflies."

"How did butterflies get in my stomach?" she asked.

"They weren't really butterflies," I explained. "It just felt like butterflies flying around your stomach."

"Well," she said, "I wish I had known they were butterflies because I would have opened my mouth and let them out."

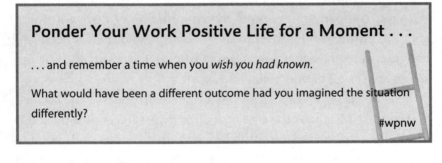

Ponder Your Work Positive Life for a Moment . . .

. . . and remember a time when you *wish you had known*.

What would have been a different outcome had you imagined the situation differently?

#wpnw

See How It Works?

You were born to believe, not bend to ego, so that you can be at your best and imagine your work positive lifestyle. Imagination is your pilot through the Skies of Unfamiliar. It is the jet fuel of how you work positive. It propels you off the runway of the negative world and takes you into the stratosphere of believing that all things are possible as the tail wind of resources converge behind you and send you soaring.

Think about how you do business this way: You focus your thoughts on the positive strengths of your business, accepting the unfamiliar changes, and filter out the negative characteristics. Next you cooperate with a team of positive persons whom you've chosen to attract, who compare and compete rarely, and you complement one another quite well, confirming, validating, and expanding positivity throughout your business. Then Team (Company Name Here) Positive—customers and clients, employees and suppliers alike—believe together that your business can grow in phenomenal ways, and begin to imagine a broader range of positive solutions you can offer and achieve based on your work positive lifestyle.

See how it works?

Imagination is the key to your work positive business success. You perceive, conceive, and believe based on more than what you alone can see, hear, taste, touch, and smell, and primarily on what you can imagine. The impossible becomes possible. The unexpected happens. The unexplainable occurs and all you can do is shrug, and say to your partners, "All I know is it actually happened."

Your company's success is the culmination of how you think about it, partner with others to think about it, and then collectively imagine outcomes that seem unrealistic at the moment, but are achievable as all of you believe.

For instance, you have picked up an acorn before and looked at it, right? It is about the size of a dime. Most likely you picked it up under an oak tree. Recently, I picked up an acorn under one of our oak trees. This particular tree is at least 150 years old. I stood there looking at the acorn, looking up at the tremendous oak, while wondering, "How did such a huge tree start as such a little acorn?" It defies my senses to understand or explain. I can only imagine…

Have you ever held a mustard seed in the palm of your hand? It's about the size of a pencil point. You plant that pencil-point seed and it grows into a six-foot-high bush. Who would have thought that was possible? You work positive when you believe that all the imagination you need to do the impossible is about the size of that mustard seed.

I remember watching my Great-Grandmother Frazier make yeast rolls. In fact, I have the bread bowl that she and her daughter, my Grandmother Greene, used to mix flour and milk. She would sift the flour, and add the liquid and other ingredients. Then she would open a very small packet of something magical called yeast. She dropped just a pinch or so in, an extremely small amount when compared with the flour. Next she would hand mix all of this concoction. Grabbing a handful of it, she would pat it out and put it down on the pan and let it sit.

I remember asking her, "Grandma, what's it doing?"

"It's rising, son," she said.

And I asked, "How?"

"The yeast makes it rise," she told me.

And I remember wondering, "How in the world does such a tiny amount of yeast make all that dough rise?"

Your imagination is like yeast. When you work positive, believing that your company will succeed in ways that defy your ability to logically understand, you rise to achieve time after time.

On another occasion, I remember going with my Grandfather Greene to plant corn. I was small and probably more in the way than helping, but he involved me at every step of the process. We opened fifty pound bags of corn seed to pour them into the planter mounted on the tractor. I dug my hand into the open sack, and stirred up the seed, pulling out a handful.

"Granddaddy," I said, "How can these little seeds fill this whole field with corn?"

He replied, "Son, this tiny corn seed becomes a huge corn stalk that produces more ears that contain more seeds that grow more stalks."

"But how does it do it?" I insisted.

"I don't know," he said. "I just know every time I plant these seeds, they grow."

You work positive when you imagine more than you can tangibly perceive in the typical five-senses fashion. Sometimes you just have to believe that if the impossible happened once, it will happen again . . . even if it first happened for someone else.

One of my favorite TV programs when I was growing up was "The Beverly Hillbillies." Jed Clampett was a backwoods sort of guy, living humbly in a run-down shack. He was hunting one day, shot at his prey and missed, but "up through the ground came a-bubblin' crude . . . oil, that is . . . black gold . . . Texas tea . . . ." Jed stumbled on a huge well of oil.

Now if you're Jed Clampett, do you complain about that greasy slick stuff that gets on your boots and keeps your crops from growing? Or, do you buy up all the land in the adjacent area and phone ExxonMobil?

You work positive as your imagination bubbles up and you envision business possibilities you never dreamed of, viable solutions to problems for yourself and others that can be marketed and sold. Why you might even see yourself around a cement pond!

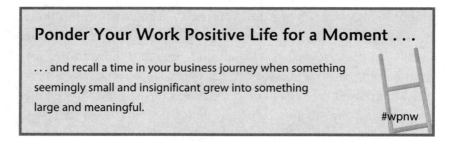

Ponder Your Work Positive Life for a Moment . . .

. . . and recall a time in your business journey when something seemingly small and insignificant grew into something large and meaningful.

#wpnw

An Apple a Day Keeps the Disbelief Away

When I speak to business groups of executives, entrepreneurs, and owners, I pass out apples to the audience. Then I ask, "How many apples are you holding in your hand?"

Of course, the first answer I get is "One" and usually the person says, "Hey, that wasn't so hard." I say, "OK, one. Anyone have another answer?"

The room gets quiet and then, usually from the back of the room, I hear someone say, "A bushel." And I ask, "How so?"

This person says, "Well, you can plant the seeds in this apple and grow a bushel of other apples."

And then I ask, "Just a bushel?"

Someone else answers, "No, you can get an orchard out of this apple."

"An orchard?" I say.

And then someone else says, "Oh, more than an orchard. There's an infinite number of apples in this apple."

"How's that?" I ask.

"You plant these seeds and they produce an orchard of apples. And from the seeds of those apples, you grow other orchards and those orchards grow still more orchards and pretty soon you can't count all the orchards."

You work positive when you imagine that you hold in your hand everything and even more than you could ever want to enjoy the work positive lifestyle. When bent to ego, you hold only what you see, hear, taste, touch, and smell—the dimensions of your company that you perceive you can influence, control, and manipulate. Your business holds so much more in store for you . . . if you will only believe that your focused, filtered, positive thoughts, conceived in a complementary relationship, can produce an infinite harvest.

You plant these seeds of success in your business and water, fertilize, cultivate, and get adequate sun to them as they bravely push up through the soil. But do you actually make the seed grow? Or, do you provide the conditions for a miracle to happen?

One of my favorite movie series is the *Indiana Jones* one. It reminds me of the westerns my Dad, brother, and I enjoyed watching on Saturdays—they are filled with life-threatening danger, there is always a woman involved, and the good guy wins.

There is one particular scene toward the end of one movie in the series that I love to recall. Indiana Jones is pursuing an artifact known as the Holy Grail. It is the cup that Jesus drank from at what is known as the Last Supper. Indy has endured every kind of danger known to humanity, but he, his hat, and his bullwhip have made it through to this last test.

He stands on the edge of a bottomless pit. The pit separates him from the Holy Grail, yet he is close enough to see it. His clue indicates that if he believes, the way to the Chalice will appear to him. Everything he sees tells him that he will plunge to his death should he step off the precipice.

Indiana Jones decides that he has come too far not to believe, so he closes his eyes, fully expecting to fall to his death, and yet he still takes that first step forward. When he does, much to his surprise, a bridge to the other side appears under his feet. Rather than dying, he runs across, seizes the cup, and returns safely.

The First Step Away Is the Hardest

Just like with Indiana Jones, that first step away from what you think you know to what you believe is the hardest.

You work positive when you believe that tiny acorns become huge oak trees, small mustard seeds become great bushes, pinches of yeast make wonderful rolls, a little corn seed produces bushels of ears, a trivial bubbling up of crude oil is worth buying a farm over, and a single apple has within it an infinite number of apples. You work positive when you imagine that the first step you take away from what you know to what you believe will literally cause the ground to rise up underneath your feet. This first step is how you redefine your reality and fulfill your dreams.

For your business to achieve its full potential, you must imagine it at its very best. As I've coached business executives, entrepreneurs, and owners through the years, I've discovered that the mundane minutia of running a business can consume most of their time, energy, and attention, leaving none for imagining possibilities beyond the current reality. If you keep doing what you've always done, you'll get what you've always got. How's that working for you? Is that how you work positive in today's rapidly changing economic environment?

Can you relate? Of course you can.

Then let's take a few minutes to imagine your business is achieving more, accomplishing what might seem impossible now, but what will soon appear normal. Most of my clients find this exercise works best with the door shut, the Blackberry turned off, and the desk phone on "Do Not Disturb." (Yes, it's that important . . .)

In Figure 12.1, three simple yet profound questions guide your imagining.

FIGURE 12.1

1. If I handed you a magic wand to wave, and money were no object, what would your business look like today?_____

_____

A. Imagine your employees. How many are there? _____

_____

What are their core values, priorities, and unique contributions?

_____

What do they tell their spouses about working for you? _____

_____

B. Imagine your customers and clients. How many are there? __

_____

What solutions are you providing them? _____

_____

What do they say to their friends when talking about you and your business? _____

_____

FIGURE 12.1, continued

C. Imagine your suppliers and vendors. How many are there? __

_____

How do they offer to help you achieve your company dreams?

_____

What do they tell their supervisors about you? _____

_____

2. What is your current reality of doing business? _____

_____

Answer as you best understand your company today.

A. Employees _____

_____

B. Customers and clients _____

_____

C. Suppliers and vendors _____

_____

3. Name three actions you can take in the next 21 days to close the gap between how you imagined your business and your current reality.

Action 1/Week 1: _____

_____

Action 2/Week 2: _____

_____

FIGURE 12.1, continued

Action 3/Week 3: _____

_____

What will be different about your company at the end of week 3?

_____

How will it more closely resemble your redefined business reality in item 1? _____

_____

Grab & Go

Remember—It's "Best to Imagine" how you work positive and that:

1. Fence posts grow into trees.

2. Tiny acorns grow sky-high oak trees.

3. Pencil-point mustard seeds grow head-tall bushes.

4. Black gold bubbles up from the hunting grounds of your business, just like it did for Jed Clampett.

5. An apple seed grows an infinite number of apples.

6. A pinch of yeast rises a pan of rolls.

7. The ground literally rises up beneath your feet when you keep your eyes on the prize of your business success.

"I ACHIEVE the POSITIVE at Work"

CHAPTER 13

"I Achieve"

*I've come to believe that all my past failure and frustration were
actually laying the foundation for the understandings that
have created the new level of living I now enjoy.*

—Tony Robbins

A woman drove down a heavily traveled street one afternoon
after getting off work a little early. The radio was blasting
her favorite song, when suddenly her car quit. She managed
to steer it over to the side of the street. She got out and looked under
the hood, not really knowing what she was searching for, but it just
seemed the thing to do.

An unfamiliar voice behind her said, "Lady, do you need some
help?" She wheeled around to discover three young men standing
behind her.

"Uh, no. Everything is fine," she said. "I'm calling AAA.
They're on their way."

"You don't need to call anyone," one of the young men said,
and grabbed her phone. The next thing she knew, she was on the
ground, trying to cover her face and protect herself from the strong-
armed blows pummeling her face first, then her stomach. Then kick

after kick broke her ribs. She lost consciousness as blood oozed from her lips.

No one saw anything as the three young men managed to start the vehicle and drove away.

About a half-hour later, a highly esteemed and successful business man was being driven down that same street in his limo. His driver slowed down when he spotted the woman lying on the sidewalk. He could see the pool of blood.

"Mr. James, there's a woman bleeding badly on the sidewalk over here. I'm going to get out and check on her," the driver said.

"No, you're not," Mr. James yelled back. "If I'm not at this meeting on time, I'll lose this loan. Drive on . . . now!"

"Can I at least call it in to 911?" the driver asked.

"Of course not," Mr. James said. "Then we'll have to come back and waste our time giving a statement. Turn left at the next intersection and take a back street to The Courtyard."

A few minutes later, an ethics professor from the local university stopped at the traffic light near where the woman was on the sidewalk, still bleeding. He peered through his windshield, not sure at first what he was seeing.

"That couldn't be a woman down on the sidewalk, could it?" he wondered. He slowly pulled away from the traffic light and stared at her, noticing the fresh pool of blood.

"It is, and she's bleeding profusely," he said out loud. "I'd better stop," and he slowed down to pull over and then thought better of it.

"Her attackers may still be around and assault me if I get out to help," he decided. He sped away, turning off the street, just in case the criminals were watching.

Just then a Latino construction worker pulled up to the traffic light. His beat-up work truck just barely kept running while waiting for the light to change. He tapped out a back-beat on his steering wheel, glad to have the truck to himself so he could listen to his music.

His glance fell on what looked like someone lying on the sidewalk. Not waiting for the light to change, he checked the intersection, and pulled quickly over to the curb beside where the woman was lying half dead. He jumped out of the truck and ran to her side.

"Hey lady! Are you OK?" he asked.

She only moaned, and tried to cover her face with her arms.

"I don't have a cell phone," he told her. He stood there, then started pacing, trying to figure out what to do.

"Lady," he said, "I'm going to put you in my truck and take you to the hospital, OK?" And with that, he picked up the woman in her blood-stained dress, and gently placed her on the passenger seat in his truck, carefully shutting the door. He ran around to the driver's side, jumped in, and sped off down the street toward Mercy General.

Screeching in on two wheels, he pulled up to the Emergency Department door. He jumped out and ran in and screamed, "Somebody come help. A woman has been attacked."

A man and a woman flew out the door, one of them screaming, "Bring a gurney and prep a room stat." They gingerly lifted the woman from the truck, placed her on the stretcher, and wheeled her inside.

The Latino construction worker followed closely behind, but when he tried to follow her through the trauma room doors, a loud voice stopped him: "Sir, I must talk with you first."

He pivoted over to the woman at the desk who said to him, "Sir, you must secure payment for our services before we can treat her. This is a private hospital, not one of the county facilities."

Incredulous, the man said, "I just found her on the street. I don't know her."

"I'm sorry, sir," the woman continued. "Our rules are clear. You either secure payment now or take her somewhere else."

The Latino construction worker straightened himself up and said, "I will gladly pay for your services."

He pulled his wallet out and handed her his medical insurance card, not knowing how he would explain this to his boss, but knowing what he had to do. "And here," he said, handing her his credit card. "Whatever else it costs that my insurance doesn't cover, you can put on my card."

Now which of these three—the businessman, the ethics professor, or the Latino construction worker—would you say makes positive things happen; achieves a work positive life?

Knowing how to perceive your business as positive in this negative world, focusing on the positive while avoiding just the "familiar" and then filtering for the positive is the first step to enjoying a work positive lifestyle. The second step is to conceive your company as positive. You cooperate with and surround yourself with positive employees and vendors, customers and clients who complement what you perceive. The third step is to redefine your notion of business reality and believe that your company can be positive, even in a negative world, avoiding your bent to ego and imagining the very best, thus making it possible for your dreams to come true.

The fourth step is about how you achieve business success through a work positive lifestyle; how you can manifest all of the previous internal work of perceive, conceive, and believe, and then externally achieve a work positive company even while doing business in a negative world. This step is the physical dynamic of how you work positive.

CHAPTER 14

Pay Attention to What's Important

Working in an office with an array of electronic devices is like trying to get something done at home with half a dozen small children around. The calls for attention are constant.

—Marilyn vos Savant

It's a big world out there. Especially when you're a child.

So when our younger daughter came home from second grade one day all excited about a science experiment, I listened carefully.

"Daddy, it was so cool," she said. "Did you know that a magnet can pick up a nail through a glass jar?"

"Really?" I said.

"It sure can. The magnet picks up the nail through the side of the jar, but it won't pick up the jar," she said.

"Now why is that?" I said.

"Because the nail is attracted to the magnet and the glass isn't."

"What do you mean 'attracted'?" I said.

"That means the nail wants to come to the magnet and the glass doesn't," she explained. "That's why the magnet can pick up the nail."

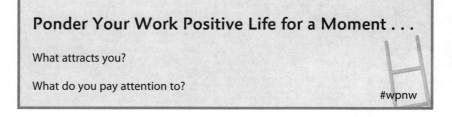

Ponder Your Work Positive Life for a Moment . . .

What attracts you?

What do you pay attention to?

#wpnw

A whole new world opened up for her in that one simple classroom experience. She discovered the attraction factor—a universal principle among people and physical objects.

There Are Lots of Attractions at Work

At what point do attractions—physical things to which we give our attention—become distractions?

Over the years of coaching executives, entrepreneurs, and owners, I have observed something: When a child—let's call him "Johnny"—cannot seem to sit still in his school desk and focus, we run him through a battery of tests, label him "ADD" or "ADHD" or some other alphabet soup name, and medicate him with a drug like Ritalin.

When Johnny graduates and grows up, sitting still in his desk long enough to finish an MBA, we stick him in an office, surrounded by concrete and glass, and encourage him to multitask. That means he can't sit still at his desk and focus on one assignment at a time. Everything is now important to Johnny. So while he is conferencing with Asia, he is also answering an e-mail from a customer in Florida, sending a text to a vendor in Texas, completing a spreadsheet to upload into PowerPoint to present at the conference, and his wife is on hold, wondering if he will make it to his 7-year-old daughter's dance recital that evening. We even reward Johnny financially when he is better than anyone else at multitasking all of these "important" tasks. So what we medicated Johnny for in elementary school, we give him a raise for as an adult.

How does that make for a work positive lifestyle?

Is this the way Johnny ultimately achieves positive business success?

Recent studies indicate that personal productivity diminishes precipitously when we multitask, as we divide our attention between too many sources, all clamoring for the gift of our focus. We get less done when we try to do more all at once.

But Then You Knew That . . .

You choose to work positive so you focus and filter for positive thoughts which means you pay attention to what is important. By paying attention to what is positively important, you begin to achieve a work positive lifestyle even though the negative world is filled with distractions of other people telling you what is important.

The only way for you to achieve what others consider impossible, but what you believe can be done because you have perceived and conceived it, is to pay attention to what is important. It's a matter of priority.

File that statement under "Easier said than done," right? If you're like most businesspeople, your productivity quotient follows the 80/20 rule—about 20 percent of what you pay attention to on any given day contributes 80 percent to your revenue. Based on my own experience in business and coaching executives, entrepreneurs, and owners, the heavy dependence on technology-driven tools today pushes these percentages closer to 90/10. For most of us running companies, we allow others to set our agenda. Technology drives minutia on steroids careening onto our field of play, and all of it is marked "urgent."

If you truly want to work positive and achieve the redefined reality of your company and fulfill your goals and dreams, you simply must pay attention to what is most important.

When I first started quail hunting, I would get really excited when a large covey of birds flew up. I remember thinking, "Wow!

With that many birds flying, I can't miss!" I would shoot into the covey without really aiming at any bird in particular. Every time I did, I missed.

Later, I learned to select one bird, focus my aim on that one bird in the covey, follow it with my gun, and shoot just at that one bird. Most of the time, I downed a bird.

Life Is Really Busy for Us Today

Despite the fact that we have fast food and instant coffee and next-day delivery when it "absolutely, positively has to be there overnight," it seems that we never quite complete our to-do list. There are perpetual coveys of tasks flying in your face all at once. How do you focus on one priority task—the most important—take aim, and fire away with your attention and achieve a work positive lifestyle in this negative world?

My Grandfather Greene told me stories of his childhood when he got up at 4:30 DP . to bring in the wood he had split previously, put it in the "cook stove" (not the stove that heated their home), and light the fire so his mother could prepare breakfast. The most important meal of the day required someone to gather eggs in the dark laid by the hens in the chicken coop near the split wood. Of course, someone in the fall had prepared the pig for just such a morning as this. The flour which was ground from their corn was in a sack in the kitchen. It was there to make the biscuits with milk which came from their cows, also fresh that morning. About the only thing that came from the "dry goods store" was the coffee. Sure they had a lot to do every morning, but there was no discussion about what was important. The necessary tasks for eating breakfast were simply taught and done.

Your biggest morning task probably is to decide whether to stop by Starbucks or McDonald's for breakfast. That leaves you an abundance of time to do other things that are important, right?

So how is that working out for you?

How do you choose which bird to aim at? Find yourself not hitting any of them?

Just shooting into the covey of "urgent" items others put on your agenda?

At the end of the day, are you walking away from that day's covey shaking your head and asking yourself, "What did I get done today?"

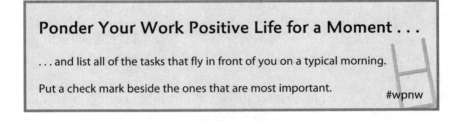

Ponder Your Work Positive Life for a Moment . . .

. . . and list all of the tasks that fly in front of you on a typical morning.

Put a check mark beside the ones that are most important.

#wpnw

What Is Important to You?

Sometimes what is really important is sacrificed on the altar of what we think is important. Resources converge in a moment and we miss it. We far too often give away our power to choose what is important to someone else and neglect the significance of the present moment in which we can truly achieve positive results and make our dreams come true.

When resources uniquely converge because the positive was perceived, conceived, and believed, someone will achieve because they acted in that present moment. Someone would have discovered the light bulb if Thomas Edison had not persevered through more than a thousand ways of not making it. Someone invested in that little startup company when it IPOed. Ever berated yourself for not buying Google on its first day? Yes, someone will act on what is important and get outstanding results. They will focus on the one bird in the covey, take aim, fire, and hit the mark. They will pay attention to what is important because they have perceived it, conceived it with another, and believed with their imagination, and they will achieve what everyone else considered impossible.

> ## Ponder Your Work Positive Life for a Moment . . .
>
> . . . and ask yourself, "Will I be that person who achieves what
> everyone else considers impossible?"   #wpnw

As you know, the negative world makes it a lot easier to not be that person. It pushes us to pay attention to the things at work that just are not that important.

When my nephew was 7 years old, he and I were watching a football game together. One of the players lost a shoe and had to leave the game.

The player came back on the field and his shoe looked…well, different. My nephew said something about it and I looked more carefully. The player was in such a hurry to get back on the field that the athletic trainer didn't have time to tape the shoe back on, securing it up his ankle. So the guy runs back on the field to play with one shoe taped up and the other untaped, which is why it looked different.

My nephew said, "I thought he had mismatched shoes on," and we laughed about it.

That same player with the different shoes ran the ball on the very next play. He broke several tackles and almost scored. My nephew said, "I guess it doesn't matter whether his shoes match or not if he can run like that."

The negative world encourages you to pay attention to the outward appearances in business like mismatched shoes. Does it really make any difference if your shoes match if you achieve positive results? When you focus your attention on making an important difference rather than avoiding being different, you perceive, conceive, and believe and thus redefine your reality. You fulfill your dreams of a redefined reality when you pay attention to what's important, not what the negative world would distract you into with its multitasking penchant.

What Is Your Positive Life Trigger?

What is your trigger for paying attention to what's important? What motivates you to give no attention to the mismatched shoes and focus on the importance of positive results?

I found my trigger some years ago. I had the opportunity to stand by an open grave as a family member was buried. His death was sudden and unexpected. As I stood there, my mind flooded with all the times I wished I had called him just to say "Hi!" Not that I had anything particular or special to say. Just "Hi!"

And then I thought about all the birthday cards I didn't send. The "just because" notes I didn't write. The times I didn't check in with him to see how life was treating him. I cried.

I decided that maybe I wasn't crying for him, but for me. For the lost opportunities while he was here. The words left unsaid. The deeds left undone.

Around that open grave that day, I noticed a dragonfly. Dragonflies are absolutely beautiful creatures. Their iridescent wings glitter in the summer sun around ponds, lakes, and wetlands all around the world. In fact, if you Google "dragonflies," you find literally thousands and thousands of websites about them, and not just university professors and naturalists sponsor these sites. There are societies of people like you and me that study dragonflies, landscape their yards to attract them, and share what they learn with others. Dragonflies inspire everything from beautiful jewelry to fairy tales. These tiny creatures' ancestry can be traced back to the beginning of time.

And yet, did you know that most dragonflies live only about a month?

So I stood there at that open grave, staring at dragonflies, and asked myself, "If I only had a month to live, what would I do?" Watching the sandy soil fill his grave and cover his casket, with dragonflies flitting about, I made a decision: I'm living differently. I am now saying all the words, some to people I haven't spoken with in 30 years. I am now doing for others rather than waiting until later.

Now I pay attention to what is important. I focus and filter for positive thoughts, avoiding just the familiar mental patterns. I go out of my way to find the unfamiliar because I'm convinced therein lies the ultimate prize. I cooperate and complement with other positive people, comparing and competing rarely. I have no Eeyore Vampires on Team Joey. I live into my birthright to believe and imagine the best every opportunity I find, steering clear of the bent to my ego. My accountability partners sniff out the trail of my ego and redirect me as necessary. I pay attention to what is important, which leads me to achieve a work positive lifestyle in this negative world—positive results like this book and the monumental transformation you're undergoing right now.

Ponder Your Work Positive Life for a Moment . . .

. . . and reflect on what you would do differently today if you discovered that you had only 30 days left to live.

#wpnw

Pay Attention to What Is Important to You

Here are a few strategies that my coaching clients and I have found particularly effective in learning to pay attention to what is important.

Start the Day Quietly

For most business persons, from the minute you walk in the building to when you crawl out at the end of the day, there is noise. Some of this noise is just part and parcel of running a business. Whatever its source, it leaves few if any moments of quiet in which to sort out important matters.

Finding a way to start your day quietly is a key to achieving your work positive lifestyle. For some executives, a quiet beginning means telling your assistant to make sure you're not disturbed. For some entrepreneurs, it means getting up before your children wake up and invade your home office. For some owners, it means you lock yourself in the building an hour before you open.

Thirty minutes to an hour seems to be an optimum time period to be quiet. During these moments of quiet, you engage in activities that coach you to sort out the negative and focus on the positive. You might read a book like this one and complete activities. You could meditate on your company's recent results and welcome unfamiliar thoughts to conceive with your employees and lead you to believe in new outcomes. You could visualize stellar success.

Your major focus at this time is to silence the noise of doing business daily and give yourself the physical space to perceive, conceive, and believe—all of which propel you to achieve positive results.

Create Boundaries

The creep of technology intrudes into all our lifestyles. Learning to work positive and pay attention to what is most important translates into daily recognizing the creep and creating boundaries that limit it.

For instance, you're in a meeting with an employee. Your desk phone rings. Do you answer it? Do you read the Caller ID window and decide?

Let's say you're working on your computer on an important project for your business. Is your e-mail open? Is it set on "automatic" so that it's making noises and popping up windows that interrupt your flow?

What if you're with a customer and your BlackBerry buzzes with a call? Do you take it?

I hope your answer is "No" in each case, but I suspect at least sometimes, it's "Yes."

Create boundaries around your technology that allow you to focus completely on what is most important. You pay for technology services. They are to serve you, not vice versa. Turn it off. After all, you're paying for it.

End Your Day with a Victory

Do you collapse into bed in total exhaustion, convinced that the rats may have won the race that day?

Do you fall asleep in front of the TV, watching the late news as you drift away?

When we discussed the importance of how to perceive a work positive lifestyle, I noted that your mind is constantly processing, even in your sleep. This means that whatever you go to sleep thinking about is what your mind spends the overnight working on.

Negative problems at work invade your dreams.

Negative economic indicators, murders, floods, and other disasters enter your mental processor for overnight delivery.

And you wonder why you're exhausted when you wake up?

Proactively program your mind to pay attention overnight to the important, positive matters of the day. A great sales day. A deal done well. A new relationship with a preferred vendor. A new employee with outstanding credentials. The fact that you kept the doors open one more day.

Sure, some work days seem to offer only the negative, but if you can focus and filter until you reach at least one positive reality from the day, and pay attention to that as you fall asleep, you'll be absolutely amazed by how refreshed you'll awaken the next morning and how much easier it will be to pay attention to the 20 percent of highly productive tasks waiting for you.

The Greatest Challenge

My greatest challenge in paying attention to what is important is actually doing just that and not just intending to do it. It's a lot easier to talk about paying attention—starting each day quietly, creating boundaries around technology, and ending each day with a victory—than it is to actually do it. I have discovered that intention is the road to nowhere. I have gone down that road before and found myself at a dead end.

I bet you have, too. So what do we do about it?

Grab & Go

In a world that's constantly buzzing, ringing, and playing song snippets, remember to "Pay Attention to What's Important" and keep in mind that:

1. We get less done when we try to do more all at once, just like Johnny.

2. If you are unsure of which bird to aim at, you hit nothing.

3. The outward appearance of your shoes is insignificant as long as you run well.

4. Go stand before an open grave today. Then decide what's important to you.

5. Start your day quietly.

6. Create boundaries around technology.

7. End your day with victory.

CHAPTER 15

Remember–Intention Is the Road to Nowhere

"Leaders, whether in the family, in business, in government or in education, must not allow themselves to mistake intentions for accomplishments."

—Jim Rohn

A business owner had two employees. He received a call from the cleaning service saying that they could not get someone to the building to clean that week due to the snow. All their employees were doing snow removal around the city in response to the blizzard.

"No problem," the owner said. "We can do it."

So he called one of his two employees into his office. "Tom, the cleaning service can't get here this week. So we're all going to pitch in and do a little cleaning. How about you clean the bathroom? All the supplies are in there."

Tom replied, "Boss, I really don't want to. My wife makes me clean the toilets at home and I absolutely hate it." And he walked out.

Later Tom thought more about the owner's request and decided that if he could clean the bathroom at home, he could do it at work.

It was not that big a deal. Besides there was no shower at work. So he did it.

When Tom refused to clean the bathroom, the owner called Ralph, the other employee, into his office. "Ralph, the cleaning service can't get here this week. So we're all going to pitch in and do a little cleaning. How about you clean the bathroom? All the supplies are in there."

"Sure thing, boss. I'll be glad to," Ralph said.

Ralph never cleaned the bathroom.

Which employee would you want on your team—Tom or Ralph?

Ponder Your Work Positive Life for a Moment . . .

When did you say "No" to someone and then went ahead and did it anyway?

And when did you say "Yes" and decided not to do it?

#wpnw

A Story of Two Employees

Which one, Tom or Ralph, achieved positive results? Which one intended to?

Our intentions—our stated desire of "I want to" or "I didn't mean to"—are pathways to our achieving positive results, but cannot be equated with achievement. "I want to" or "I didn't mean to" does nothing to change the outcome or the results. Intentions, in and of themselves, are the road to nowhere.

You can perceive the positive at work. Then you can conceive it—confirm, validate, and expand it—with other positive people in your business, employees and vendors, customers and clients. You can believe it with every fiber of your being and imagine the best possible positive results for your company. You can even decide to pay attention to what is most important about your business. However, if you just intend to act on it, you will never achieve a work positive lifestyle in this negative world.

For example, I was talking with one of those friends I mentioned earlier that I had not seen in over 30 years. She asked me what I do for fun and I said, "Well, I really enjoy running a mile on a treadmill at the fitness center and working out on the Nautilus machines. My daughter goes along in her off season from track and so that's a lot of fun."

My friend was quiet for a moment and then said, "I do that in my mind, and know I should go, but somehow never quite make it to the gym."

Intention is the road to nowhere. It's the pathway to not quite making it to the gym.

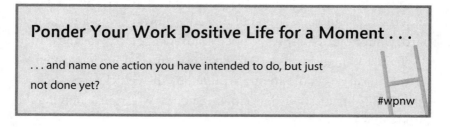

Ponder Your Work Positive Life for a Moment . . .

. . . and name one action you have intended to do, but just not done yet?

#wpnw

Intention in Isolation

As we discover in the next chapter, intention can be a powerful catalyst when combined with attention and action. However, like all catalysts, when isolated, intention is ineffective in producing a reaction of any kind, much less a desirable one.

So how do you recognize isolated intention? How do you know when your intention is just that—only an intention with no connection to attention or action? What does intention by itself act like?

Intention Is a Burden

When isolated, instead of empowering you to achieve positive results, intention burdens you and slows you down from achieving positive results at work. One summer, on Lake Isabella, located in the high desert an hour east of Bakersfield, California, some folks, new to boating, were having a problem. They couldn't get their brand-new 22-footer going no matter how hard they tried. It was so sluggish in almost every maneuver, no matter how much they opened up the throttle.

After about an hour of trying to make it go, they putted to a nearby marina, thinking someone there could tell them what was wrong. They found someone who did a thorough topside check that found everything in perfect working condition. The engine ran fine, the outdrive went up and down, the prop was the correct size and pitch.

So, one of the marina guys jumped in the water to check underneath, and came up choking on water, he was laughing so hard. Under the boat, still strapped securely in place, was the trailer.

Think of intention as that trailer. It has no propulsion system of its own. It carries your attention, pulled by the vehicle of action. But in and of itself, it is a burden, slowing you down from achieving the impossible so you can work positive.

Ponder Your Work Positive Life for a Moment . . .

What is your trailer or burden of something undone that you are attached to?

#wpnw

Intention Seeks Perfection Immediately

When separated from attention and action, intention not only weighs you down, it also seeks perfection immediately. You want to do something perfectly right now without giving the requisite time and attention to accrue in preparation for action. For your business, mistakes are fatal. Your employees know it because you don't tolerate anything that smells like a mistake. Your customers and clients know it because even when you make one, you won't admit it. You'll blame everyone else—even your employees—before you'll take responsibility for it.

I can relate. I wanted to learn to play the guitar when I was a teenager. I saved some money, bought a guitar, and took lessons.

The guitar was beautiful, nothing extravagant, but it was at least a music store guitar and not a "dime store" guitar like some of my friends had. It sounded beautiful when my instructor played it . . . but it sounded a little different when I played it. I just couldn't make the music come out of the guitar that my teacher did. I practiced for hours, trying not to make mistakes, which meant that I'd get to the same place in a song and make the same mistake every time. My teacher said, "Everybody makes mistakes. That's the way we learn." All I learned was that my favorite group, the Eagles, would never discover me.

However, I finally learned to play "House of the Rising Sun" with no mistakes, but that was the only song I ever played, because I couldn't stand the mistakes of trying to learn another song. Eventually I put the guitar down and never picked it up again. It's in my brother's basement today.

Since then I've learned that my teacher was right. The only people who aren't making mistakes are either dead or, like I did, quit trying. Everybody makes mistakes, and we can learn from them.

I intended to learn to play the guitar, but my bent to ego—my perfectionism—got in the way. Or, to put it another way, I divorced my intention to play the guitar from giving my attention to it and action with it.

Intention Fears Failure

Intention is the road to nowhere. Not only does it burden us and seek perfection, it also fears failure.

For so many executives, entrepreneurs, and business owners, fear of failure paralyzes. It's why they analyze an opportunity until it's gone with no positive results. So many successful businessmen and women tell their stories of success, but virtually every one has several chapters of failed previous attempts. Work positive devotees understand that failure is an experience, not a person.

On New Year's Day, 1929, Georgia Tech played UCLA in the Rose Bowl. In that game, Roy Riggles recovered a fumble for UCLA. Riggles became confused and ran 65 yards in the wrong direction. One of his teammates outran him and tackled him just before he scored for the other team. When UCLA tried to punt, Tech blocked the kick and scored a safety.

That strange play came in the first half, and everyone watching the game was asking the same question: What will Coach Price do with Roy Riggles in the second half? Price said, "Men, the same team that played the first half starts the second."

"Coach," Riggles said, "I can't do it. I couldn't face that crowd in the stadium to save my life."

Then Price said, "Roy, get up and go on back out there. The game is only half over."

Coach Price understood that failure is a play in the game, not the game itself.

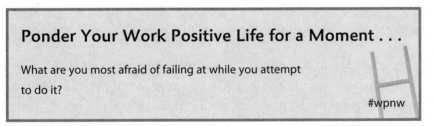

Ponder Your Work Positive Life for a Moment . . .

What are you most afraid of failing at while you attempt to do it?

#wpnw

Intention Gives Up and Quits

Excuses for not achieving positive results in our businesses arise from our fear of failure. We intend to do something, but fear we will fail, forgetting that failure is not fatal or that the game is not over. When you truly perceive, conceive, and believe in the positive aspects of your company despite the negative context in which you do business, failure is actually not an option. You choose to perceive a positive vision of a redefined reality for your corporation, surround yourself with a team of positive people with whom to test the vision, and hold fast to the belief that you are supported in your perception, plus you get constant feedback once you get started. Positive achievement, while messy sometimes, is accomplished. Remember the daylilies and birds? While a positive outcome may not be guaranteed, it is assured to occur, albeit possibly in a way other than the one you originally perceived.

This assurance means that the role of intention becomes one of continuing the pursuit even when the path zigs and zags. Perseverance is the key. When isolated from attention and action, intention gives up rather than continues the pursuit.

Walter Johnson was a legendary baseball pitcher, a pitching phenomenon in his time, striking out batters at will.

A rookie faced Johnson for the very first time. Before he knew what happened, the rookie had two strikes called on him. He just shook his head and walked away.

The umpire took off his mask and called after the rookie, "Son, where are you going? That was just strike two."

"You keep the third strike," the rookie said. "I've seen enough."

It happens, doesn't it? You see enough at work and you just want to walk away and just want to say to your employees and vendors, customers and clients, bankers and attorneys, "You keep it."

There is something to be said for staying in the batter's box, even when you think you'll strike out. When you walk away, you learn nothing except how to quit. When you persevere, you learn something—about yourself, about the situation, and what it takes to achieve positive results in your business.

Intention Underestimates the Power of One

Intention is the road to nowhere, to walking away when it is divorced from attention and action. Alone, it underestimates the power you have as one person who perceives, conceives, and believes a work positive lifestyle in the negative world.

But maybe that's a real challenge for you to believe—that you as one person can have the effect of transforming the world around you. Do you ever wonder if what you do through your business matters? That is, do you ever ask yourself if your work actions—the actions of one person leading a company—make a difference?

I traveled to do some coaching with an executive in his context, and while in this particular city, something unusual happened. It seems that a city employee accidentally spilled some hydraulic oil into the city's water supply. An emergency bulletin was broadcast, letting us all know that while we could bathe, we couldn't drink the water even if we boiled it.

I didn't think much about it until I went to lunch and discovered that I could only order bottled water. That evening I found that homemade bread wasn't available until just before we sat down to eat. The next morning we couldn't get coffee at the coffee shop. Bottles and jugs of water flew off store shelves, even selling out in some places.

One person's adventure in learning how to keep hydraulic oil out of the water supply paralyzed a major metropolitan area for most of a day, transforming the way we ate, drank, and even bathed. Intention—"I didn't mean to spill the oil"—had no effect whatsoever on the outcome of this one person's action. It was separated from attention and action. Intention by itself underestimates the power of one person to change the lives of others.

Ponder Your Work Positive Life for a Moment . . .

What have you perceived, conceived, and believed that you could achieve, but refused to pursue because you are "just one person"?

#wpnw

Intention Rushes to Results

Are you beginning to understand now why intention alone is the road to nowhere for your company? What you wanted to do or meant to do at work but did not actually do burdens you and prevents you from achieving positive results. It seeks perfection immediately, short-circuiting your learning the unfamiliar. It fears failure, which shuts your action down, causing you to give up. It underestimates the power that you as one person have to transform the lives of your customers by solving their problems.

Occasionally, intention does draw a bead on the bull's-eye of active results, but because it is divorced from attention, whatever action it prompts impatiently rushes to results. Your attention is short-circuited. You lack sufficient information to inform your actions.

I enjoy growing roses and was admiring my rose bushes one day. A few days later, I noticed that almost all the blooms had faded and that even though there were plenty of buds, there just weren't any open flowers.

I thought, "I wish these rose buds would hurry up and open, or, at least part of them. I wish there was something I could to do to speed them up."

Then it occurred to me that there is no way to unfold a rose bud more quickly without destroying it. Sure, I can water it regularly and feed it often, but I simply destroy a rose bud when I attempt to open it with my hands. The rose bush is damaged when rushed.

Separated from attention and action, intention rushes you through your business at times—through tough times or easy times or all the times in between. However, you damage your business growth when you rush it.

In fact, as you perceive, conceive, and believe during such times of danger and opportunity for your company, you begin to achieve dynamic results of growth that facilitate the display of your business's best traits. Your core values, business priorities, and unique contributions that separate you from the competition shine clearly into your business relationships. It is by not rushing through negative economic conditions that the challenges of each moment present themselves as alive and vibrant opportunities destined for your work positive success. You do more than survive. You thrive.

Here's how your adverse economic context works to strengthen your business. The Great Barrier Reef stretches some 1,800 miles from New Guinea to Australia. The lagoon side of the reef looks pale and lifeless, while the ocean side is vibrant and colorful. The reason for this phenomenon is that the coral on the lagoon side is in still water with no challenge for its survival. It dies early. The coral on the ocean side is constantly being tested by wind, waves, and storms—surges of power. It fights for survival every day of its life. It changes and adapts as it is challenged and tested. It grows healthier and stronger every day.

As we learn to work positive in this negative world, we are like that coral. Our businesses come alive and grow when challenged and tested by economic storms. The untested aspects of our companies intend to grow, but unchallenged, atrophy. The challenged side confronts adversity daily and therein is its success. That which could be seen as negative—economic assault—becomes the opportunity for proving work positive competencies thrive even in what we think is the worst of times.

Here is the key to understanding the true power of intention: Left alone, unchallenged, your intention to do business in a work positive lifestyle is the road to nowhere. Partnering with attention

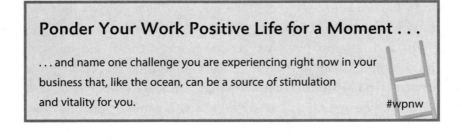

Ponder Your Work Positive Life for a Moment . . .

. . . and name one challenge you are experiencing right now in your business that, like the ocean, can be a source of stimulation and vitality for you.

#wpnw

and action, as we shall see next, intention is a powerful catalyst that, like the ocean, stimulates a positive vitality that redefines your reality and grows your company toward the fulfillment of your dreams.

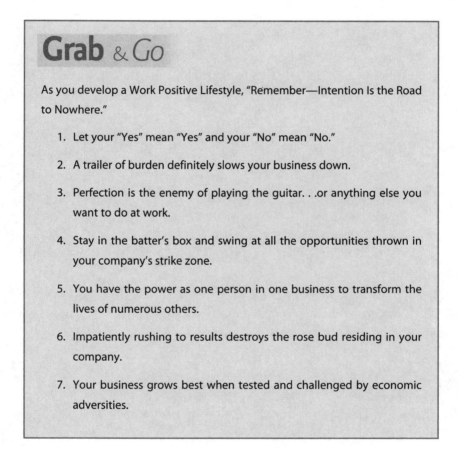

Grab & Go

As you develop a Work Positive Lifestyle, "Remember—Intention Is the Road to Nowhere."

1. Let your "Yes" mean "Yes" and your "No" mean "No."

2. A trailer of burden definitely slows your business down.

3. Perfection is the enemy of playing the guitar. . .or anything else you want to do at work.

4. Stay in the batter's box and swing at all the opportunities thrown in your company's strike zone.

5. You have the power as one person in one business to transform the lives of numerous others.

6. Impatiently rushing to results destroys the rose bud residing in your company.

7. Your business grows best when tested and challenged by economic adversities.

CHAPTER 16

Take the Prescription for Achievement

"Action is the foundational key to all success."

—Pablo Picasso

O ne summer, I decided that the shrubs at one end of our home had grown too tall. I decided to cut them back, down to a stump.

I got out the chainsaw and cut back the shrubs. It took a while because they were tall and thick, but eventually I got down to the main trunk. All I left was a stump.

Our daughters asked, "Daddy, why did you kill the bushes?"

"I didn't kill them. I cut them back," I said.

"No, Daddy, you killed them."

"Watch them," I said. "Soon you'll see tiny green shoots coming out of them. And by this time next year, they'll be covered with greenery."

"No, they won't, Daddy. You killed them."

Well, the next spring arrived, and slowly but surely, green shoots emerged from those dead stumps. Just a few at first, then more, and soon they were full.

The shrubs survived and thrived.

When you attempt to achieve positive results in your business merely by intention, you are like those shrubs I cut back. You appear dead. You look around work and wonder why the economic conditions mowed you down, what you did to deserve such a slow sales period. You search for someone to blame—your employees, your customers, your clients, your vendors, the President and Congress. You avoid taking personal responsibility for your lack of attention and action because your bent to ego does not tolerate such imperfection. You compare your business to others and compete with them in an effort to fortify your deficit of positive results. "At least my business is better off than theirs," you tell yourself. You retreat into your familiar perceptions and take solace in your memories that once upon a time you succeeded.

As we discovered in the last chapter, intention is merely a catalyst. It requires attention and action to interact with it so you can achieve the impossible positive results you originally perceived, conceived, and believed.

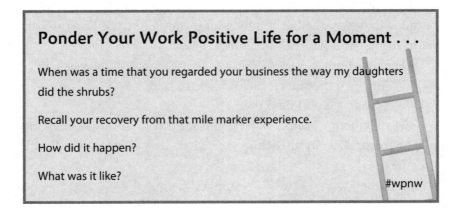

Ponder Your Work Positive Life for a Moment . . .

When was a time that you regarded your business the way my daughters did the shrubs?

Recall your recovery from that mile marker experience.

How did it happen?

What was it like?

#wpnw

The Importance of Action

Attention plus intention is an excellent beginning to achieving positive results in your company, to bringing to life what you perceive as positive, conceive with other positive people, and believe will happen as you imagine the very best for your business. However, there is still one missing ingredient in your prescription for achieving your redefined reality. That missing element is action.

Action brings achievement. Perhaps you have read these universal truths before:

"Ask and you'll receive."

"Knock and it'll open."

"Seek and you'll find it."

Each one of them begins with an active verb. You have to do something to get the positive results you desire.

What if these statements read:

"Sit there with your mouth closed, expect people to read your mind, and you'll receive."

"Just stand there, staring at the door, and it'll open for you."

"Relax in your favorite recliner and see what shows up on your front porch."

Sure you may be giving some attention to the situation, and I am sure you intend to do something about it. However, unless you act—create some movement, get some traction—you fail to redefine your reality and fulfill your dreams for your work positive lifestyle.

The Prescription for Achieving Your Work Positive Lifestyle

Here's the prescription for enjoying your work positive lifestyle once you perceive, conceive, and believe:

Attention + Intention + ACTION = Achievement of the
Work Positive Lifestyle

What you once considered impossible for your business becomes possible when you live into this prescription.

As you discovered earlier, attention is that attraction factor for your mental energy of perception. Not only do you focus and filter your thoughts, you concentrate them on an identified business priority, doing so along with conceiving employees and vendors, customers and clients with whom you share a belief that this reality can be redefined, that dream can truly be fulfilled. Intention is that catalyst that carries your attention like a trailer does a boat to the vehicle that energizes them both into forward motion. So you can put your attention (the boat) on the trailer of your intention, and connect them both (or hook onto the bumper hitch of the truck) to action.

The Impossible Becomes Possible When You Act

I drove to the Washington, DC, area to do a speaking engagement. I left early, knowing that traffic in Northern Virginia would slow me down. I had no idea how slow that would be until I arrived on a major highway that quickly became a parking lot. Road construction all around us pushed traffic from many lanes to a couple.

As I sat in traffic, I looked up into my rearview mirror. I saw a huge motor grader heading toward me. It was one of those vehicles that carry ten tons or more of dirt from one place to another. It kept coming toward me and was not turning. It filled my rearview mirror. Soon all I could see was the front of this huge dirt mover.

I started imagining what would be said at my funeral—"He was a good man who didn't have sense enough to get out of the way of a motor grader"—and what the headlines would read—"Author Buried Under Ten Tons of Dirt in Construction Accident."

At what seemed to me the last possible moment, that gigantic earth mover turned off to the right, onto the lane under construction, and continued another couple of hundred yards and stopped. I breathed a prayer of thanks, and then looked closely at the massive machinery. A door opened on the tiny cab and out popped a guy who was about five foot, two inches tall, and probably weighed 140 pounds dripping wet.

The thought ran through my mind: "If I asked a group of people if a 140-pound man could move singlehandedly 10 tons of dirt, most of them would respond, 'No way.' And yet he did the impossible."

This guy lived into the prescription for working positive:

Attention + Intention + ACTION = Achievement

and I am very grateful he did.

If he can achieve those positive results, if he can transform the impossible into the possible, if he can redefine reality and fulfill his dreams, so can you.

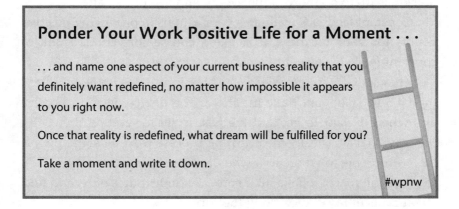

Ponder Your Work Positive Life for a Moment . . .

. . . and name one aspect of your current business reality that you definitely want redefined, no matter how impossible it appears to you right now.

Once that reality is redefined, what dream will be fulfilled for you?

Take a moment and write it down.

#wpnw

How Do You Act Best?

I imagine you are wondering, "How can I take action to redefine reality and fulfill my dreams in such a negative world and avoid perceiving just familiar thoughts, comparing and competing with others, bending to ego, and simply intending to act?"

I understand. I am right there with you. Here are two keys:

1. Listen to constant feedback, and;
2. Work positive regardless.

Listen to Constant Feedback

Think of constant feedback as the results of your action. When you avoid perceiving just familiar thoughts, you march off your mental map into what is uncharted territory. When you compare and compete rarely, you cease using Eeyore Vampires as a reference point and instead conceive positively with others, listening carefully to their confirmation, validation, and expansion of your positive perceptions about your company. When you move away from your bent to ego, you begin to imagine the best possible business scenarios by living into your birthright to believe. As you act on the positive results you perceive, conceive, and believe, you discover that some of your actions produce dramatic results in your bottom line. You also discover some ways of doing business that do not work so well. You quickly learn to do more of the former and less of the latter.

Constant feedback evaluates your actions in producing positive results for your business. It is like a course correction. Think of constant feedback as your company's GPS.

I have a GPS in our vehicles. I type in my destination and tell the GPS to "Go!" and take me there. The device decides where I am, where I want to go, and the best route for getting there. (By the way, that's basically the coaching process we are using now.) It then directs me in where and when to turn. I can program the GPS to avoid toll roads, to take interstates or scenic routes only, and find restaurants of my choice along the trip.

When I take a turn that the GPS does not recommend, it then recalculates and advises me accordingly. "Miles" (the Australian male voice on my wife's GPS) says something like, "Recalculating" or "Please make a U-turn when possible" or gives me the best street to turn on to get back on route. So far, "Miles" has yet to call me an idiot or a fool, or asked me "What were you thinking?" or "Are you asleep or stupid?" He simply recalculates and redirects.

The negative world wants you to call yourself an idiot or a fool, or ask yourself, "What was I thinking? Oh, wait, I wasn't," or, "Are you asleep or stupid?" when your efforts produce less positive results for your business.

However, instead of placing a value judgment on you or your business driving abilities, simply receive the constant feedback of those actions that are more effective than others and pursue them. Do those actions more often in your day-to-day business practices. Facilitate the results as just that—results—and feed them back into how you perceive, conceive, and believe for future company actions. Just like "Miles" suggests, "recalculate" and do what works best to get you back on the preferred path of positive results for your business despite the negative world.

Ponder Your Work Positive Life for a Moment . . .

When did you "make a mistake," learn from it, and course correct your business to a positive outcome? Name a recent "mistake" at work and perceive how you can course correct to a positive outcome.

#wpnw

Work Positive Regardless

The second important action factor, work positive regardless, comes into play next. At times we all do more than "recalculate." We allow negativity to creep into our perceiving. We invite Eeyore Vampires into the circle of people with whom we conceive. We let the "can't do its" leap into what we believe. Remember how as we compare and compete, we begin to practice "negative conceiving?" We are tempted to stop acting.

It is at this very intersection that we simply must work positive regardless, moving toward positive results no matter what. Perseverance in taking action is a key to achieving a work positive lifestyle. The longer I coach executives, entrepreneurs, and business owners, and the more I study the successful traits of those who work positive, the more convinced I become of the importance of persevering.

For instance, Abraham Lincoln went bankrupt as a business owner and lost more political elections than he won on his way to the White House and salvaging our war-torn nation. On his way to becoming what is perhaps the highest paid comedian in the world, Jerry Seinfeld forgot all his jokes the first time he did stand-up comedy, got fired from a TV show because he could not act, and had his show cancelled. Michael Jordan was cut from the basketball team at Laney High School in Wilmington, North Carolina, in his freshman year along the way to becoming what many consider the best basketball player in modern history. In creating the light bulb, Thomas Edison survived a laboratory fire that destroyed all his notes with some 1,999 ways not to make a light bulb. The country music group Alabama was dubbed an "overnight success" in the late 1970s, and yet they had been playing and touring for many years, 12 years at The Bowery in Myrtle Beach, South Carolina. John Grisham sold copies of his first book out of the trunk of his car in Charlottesville, Virginia, and other places he could drive between court cases before achieving the title of "best-selling author."

Vincent Van Gogh created 800 paintings, but sold only one in his lifetime. He died at 37, and the first one-man exhibit of his works occurred after he had died. Tom Landry, Chuck Noll, and Bill Walsh accounted for 9 of the 15 Super Bowl victories from

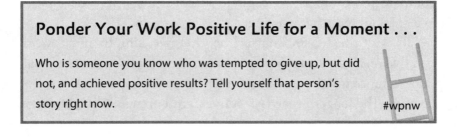

Ponder Your Work Positive Life for a Moment . . .

Who is someone you know who was tempted to give up, but did not, and achieved positive results? Tell yourself that person's story right now.

#wpnw

1974 to 1989. They also had the worst records of first-season head coaches in NFL history. Test pilot Chuck Yeager said, "I have learned to back up, but I never give up."

You can back up but not give up like Chuck Yeager and all these other persons who achieved positive results. If you truly want to work positive, you perceive, conceive, and believe in the positive factors of your business, and then you achieve the positive— redefining your reality and fulfilling your business dreams. You transform the impossible into the possible by listening to constant feedback and working positive regardless.

Achieving Your Work Positive Results

The positive results you achieve at work are astoundingly simple and profound at times.

I visited a friend with cancer in the hospital. I had just walked in when the nurse appeared in the doorway, and said to my friend, "I'm sorry, we don't have any."

My friend looked at me and said, "I'll bet you're wondering what I requested. Toothpicks. I asked if they had any toothpicks. I just love my toothpicks after I eat."

I thought to myself walking down the hall after our visit, "There she is, dying from cancer, and all she wants is a toothpick." As I rode down the elevator, the thought hit me, "Go get her a box of toothpicks. It's such a little thing."

So I went to the grocery store, bought a box of toothpicks, and went back to the hospital, where she was eating her supper, and

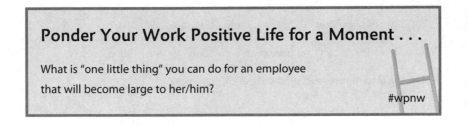

Ponder Your Work Positive Life for a Moment . . .

What is "one little thing" you can do for an employee
that will become large to her/him?

#wpnw

said, "I have just what you'll want after your meal" and handed her the toothpicks.

I will always remember her look of surprise, and her laughter. Sometimes it's the little things in life that become large when you achieve positive results.

A client's insurance agency is just a few blocks from a high school. One day, a student walked in and asked to speak with the owner. My client met her, and she said, "I'm in the Distributive Education program at my school down the street and I need a job. It has to be a job I can walk to since I'm only 15 and can't drive. You don't have to pay me. I need to work six hours a week."

He was so impressed that one so young walked right in and asked for a job that he gave it to her on the spot. "Nobody works for me for free," he told her. So he paid her for the six hours each week.

Since that day, her hours have increased as has her salary. She worked her way through high school and through college. She graduated with a degree in fashion design. Once college was only an impossible dream, but she fulfilled it. She did a design internship in Europe, finished college, and now lives in California working for a design company.

All because she paid attention to what businesses were nearby, intended to stop by, and acted by stepping through the door of my client's business and asked for a job.

A 6-year-old friend of mine discovered that I live with horses on our farm and got really excited. She asked our horses' names

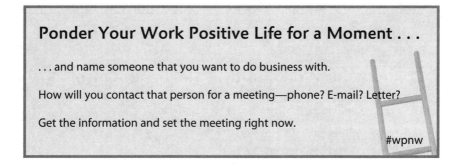

Ponder Your Work Positive Life for a Moment . . .

. . . and name someone that you want to do business with.

How will you contact that person for a meeting—phone? E-mail? Letter?

Get the information and set the meeting right now.

#wpnw

and wanted to know what they looked like. I said, "Do you like horses?"

"Yes, I do," she said. "I went to horse camp last summer."

"You did?" I said. "Was it fun?"

"You betcha," she said. "The teacher told me that it's hard to ride ponies. They're hard to handle. But they weren't hard for me. I thought they were easy."

"Why were they easy for you?" I said.

"I didn't believe the teacher. I just got on and rode," she said.

My 6-year-old friend, born to believe, chose to imagine her life at its best. For her, that meant taking the action step of riding a horse despite what the Eeyore Vampire in her life said. She achieved the impossible.

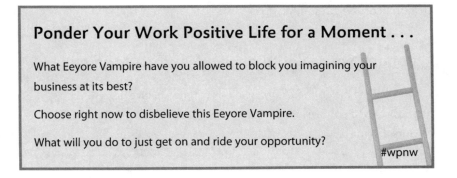

Ponder Your Work Positive Life for a Moment . . .

What Eeyore Vampire have you allowed to block you imagining your business at its best?

Choose right now to disbelieve this Eeyore Vampire.

What will you do to just get on and ride your opportunity?

#wpnw

I can still remember when our older daughter was a preschooler. She had a lot of her toys scattered on the floor. I asked her to please pick them up.

"I don't want to, Daddy," she said. "I'm too tired."

I looked at her with my "You don't really expect me to believe that" look. She looked back at me with her "Please fall for that line" look.

So I said, "Well, you will pick up your toys, but what if we play a game first?"

"OK," she said.

"What about 'Ride the horsey?'" I asked. That was her favorite game with me at the time. It's the one where you put the child on your leg and "Ride the horsey down to town, better watch out 'cause you might fall down" and then lower the child to floor.

She climbed up in my lap and rode the horsey a couple of times. Then I said, "Now clean up your toys and we'll ride the horsey one more time."

She put her toys away in about 90 seconds. Amazingly, she wasn't too tired to ride the horsey again, either.

Working positive regardless is challenging at times. Some days we face something in our businesses we had rather avoid or at least procrastinate. In those moments, it is just fine to play, and then work positive. You know what they say about "all work and no play," right? The road to redefining your reality and fulfilling your dreams can be fun, also!

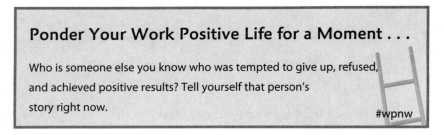

Ponder Your Work Positive Life for a Moment . . .

Who is someone else you know who was tempted to give up, refused, and achieved positive results? Tell yourself that person's story right now.

#wpnw

As you act on your business intentions to which you have given your attention, the positive results you perceived, conceived, and believed could happen actually do. Your reality redefines and then realigns so as to fulfill your business dreams. Your company positively succeeds even in a negative world.

Your business becomes so positive that you wonder, "What do I do next?"

That is when you realize that while you have taken the deliberate steps to perceive, conceive, believe, and achieve your work positive lifestyle, you have in reality received it. Out of gratitude, you now desire above and beyond anything else to help others discover how to work positive, also.

Grab & Go

"Take the Prescription for Achievement."

1. Attention + Intention + ACTION = Achievement of the Work Positive Lifestyle

2. Ask to receive. Knock to open. Seek to find.

3. A 140-pound man can move 10 tons of dirt.

4. Listen to and follow your business's work positive GPS. Then recalculate your route to success and redirect your plans.

5. Work positive regardless like Abraham Lincoln, Jerry Seinfeld, Michael Jordan, Thomas Edison, Alabama, John Grisham, Vincent Van Gogh, Tom Landry, Chuck Noll, and Bill Walsh, and Chuck Yeager.

6. Buy toothpicks for a friend. Ask for a job and go to college. Just get on the horse and ride into your company's work positive success.

7. Ride the horsey down to town first. Then pick up your toys. Play!

"I RECEIVE the POSITIVE at Work"

CHAPTER 17

"I Receive"

*"The thing that lies at the foundation of positive change,
the way I see it, is service to a fellow human being."*

—Lech Walesa

When my wife was pregnant with our first child, she really wanted a certain kind of baby crib. It even had a name—the Jenny Lind crib.

Frankly, at that point in my life, I didn't have enough money to buy it, but I really wanted to purchase it because it meant that much to my wife. I was discovering even then how to work positive. So I changed my perception, released my imagination, conceived a complementary relationship, believed that I could find the money, and acted on my attention and intention so I achieved the positive result of buying that crib.

First, I remembered my shotgun. I had not been hunting for years with that gun, but it was still special to me. Santa Claus brought it to me when I was 13 years old. It was my "dream gun"—a Remington 870 Wingmaster pump action 12 gauge with a 28-inch modified choke barrel. I drooled all over "her page" in the

Sears Wishbook catalog that year. I stood for hours staring at her in the local gun shop. Not that I was attached to my gun or anything like that . . .

Then, in a flash I decided that the crib was coming and the gun was going. I would sell my shotgun and buy the baby crib. On my way to the gun shop to sell it, I stopped by to visit my friend, James, who said he wanted it. So I sold the shotgun to him and bought the crib, presenting it to my wife as a surprise baby gift. She loved it!

About fourteen years later, on my 40th birthday, my wife threw a huge birthday party for me. She had about 250 of my closest friends over for a meal and party. It was great.

After everyone left, she escorted me into our home and said, "There's one more thing. Close your eyes and hold out your hands and I will give you a big surprise."

I did, and then she said, "OK, open your eyes! Here's your birthday present" and handed me my Remington Wingmaster 12 gauge shotgun that I had sold to buy the Jenny Lind baby crib.

"Where did you get it?" I said.

"From James," she said. "I called him and told him that you were turning 40 and asked him if I could buy your gun back. And Joey," she said. "He wouldn't let me pay him. He gave it to me as your present."

When you perceive, conceive, believe, and achieve a work positive lifestyle and give it away to others, you receive back more of the same positivity.

Knowing how to perceive a work positive lifestyle in this negative world, focusing on the positive while avoiding just the "familiar," and then placing the positive filter on your thoughts is the first step to actually enjoying your positive life. It is the mental dynamic.

The second step is to attract your work team, customers and clients, vendors and suppliers based on your core values, work priorities, and unique contribution your business makes to the world. Together you conceive how to work positive by cooperating with and surrounding yourself with these positive people who complement what you perceive. "I Conceive" is the social dynamic of enjoying a work positive lifestyle.

The third step is to redefine your reality of your company and believe that you can work positive, even in a negative world, avoid your bent to ego and imagine your business at its best. "I Believe" is the emotional dynamic of a work positive lifestyle.

The fourth step describes how you achieve—the physical dynamic—a work positive lifestyle even while living in a negative world by acting on your attention and intention. You pay attention to what's important in your company, align your intention to do something about it, and act on achieving the impossible for your employees and vendors, customers and clients.

This fifth and final section is about the unique rewards and delightful experiences you have as you work positive, sharing what you've received, even while working in a negative world. This fifth practice of "I Receive" is the ethical dynamic of how you work positive.

CHAPTER 18

Say "Thank You"

"It's nice to help remember somebody who really made
a very positive difference in the world."

—Mary Hart

O ne day, a small card showed up in the mail and found its way to my desk. I opened it and it read something like this,

Dear Dr. Joey,

You don't know me and we'll probably never meet personally. I was in the audience at a speaking engagement you did. I was a mess that day. My business was dying.

You changed my life. After listening to you, I found the way to work positive and the motivation to do it.

I just wanted to say thank you for saving my business and my life.

It took me about three tissues to get it together after reading this powerful handwritten note!

What I learned from a person I don't even remember meeting was this: two little words—"thank you"—are among the most powerful on the planet. And when they are written personally, by someone's hand holding an ink pen—instead of typed in an e-mail or text—they grow exponentially more powerful.

Yes, your work positive lifestyle transformation requires a ton of energy and effort by you to perceive, conceive, believe, and achieve the positive results you've dreamed about. But at the end of the day, you simply find a way to say "thank you" to your tour guides and fellow tourists who invested in you along the business journey because you realize that you received the positive, too.

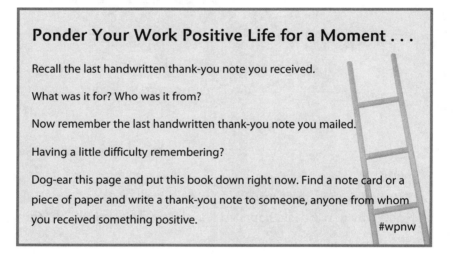

Ponder Your Work Positive Life for a Moment . . .

Recall the last handwritten thank-you note you received.

What was it for? Who was it from?

Now remember the last handwritten thank-you note you mailed.

Having a little difficulty remembering?

Dog-ear this page and put this book down right now. Find a note card or a piece of paper and write a thank-you note to someone, anyone from whom you received something positive.

#wpnw

Givers Gain®

Ivan Misner, the founder of BNI (Business Network International), created this franchised referral network of business people on the philosophy of "Givers Gain.®" That is, the universe is rooted in the eternal principle that when you give to others—in this case, when you refer business to other members in your chapter—you literally gain more business because you give.

Think about your own business for a moment. Have you ever said, "I went to help him out, and he helped me more"? Or, "I told Suzie about John and how he's a great guy to buy a car from, and six people showed up in my store the other day saying John sent them"?

It happens. Givers Gain.®

As you have begun to work positive and work into your reality these practices to perceive, conceive, believe, and achieve positive results in this negative world, you have discovered something. You have started to receive positive results.

How do you react to these positive results?

Any broken-arm back-patting going on? Sure, you have rerouted neural pathways, kicked the Eeyore Vampires to the curb, believed so intently that you imagined the best, and wedded your attention to your intention and then acted. You have experienced some positive results. You are beginning to enjoy your work positive lifestyle.

But notice how everything you have done has been guided. This book has guided you. I was guided in writing this book.

You learned how your mind works best and used it accordingly. Yet did you create your brain?

You discovered how relationships are best lived into and started doing that. Yet did you seek out all the positive people associated with your company? Most of them found you as you attracted them because you focused on and filtered for positive perceptions.

You realized that you were born to believe and could actually imagine your business at its best. And yet did you give birth to yourself?

You recognized that as you paid more attention to your perceiving, conceiving, and believing, coupled them to your intentions, and then acted on them, that positive results started showing up in your P&L, on the faces of your satisfied customers and clients, in the handwritten notes your vendor started sending, and in the looks of gratitude your employees and their families give you.

Sure, you are an integral player in the game of making these results happen, but did you act alone? Positive results showed up that are unexplainable, right?

Ultimately, you work these important first four practices to the best of your ability, but it all comes down to the simple recognition that as your reality redefines and your dreams are fulfilled, you receive your work positive lifestyle.

Ponder Your Work Positive Life for a Moment . . .

What is one positive result you received while reading this book?

#wpnw

Think about it this way. Have you ever said, "What goes around, comes around"? What did you mean by that?

Givers Gain,® right?

Have you ever said, "You reap what you sow"? What is the significance of that statement to you?

Ultimately you receive your work positive lifestyle.

These two statements describe accurately what you have done in the previous four practices. So what else can we say but "thank you" as we receive a work positive lifestyle?

Do You Say "Thank You" to Your Customers?

Once you realize that at the end of the day, or month, or fiscal year, you have received your work positive lifestyle, your attitude becomes one of gratitude. You want to say "thank you!" to someone. Have you thought about starting with your customers?

One of my favorite books is Tim Sanders' *Love Is the Killer App: How to Win Business and Influence Friends* (www.TimSanders.com). Tim's books, speaking, and consulting practice is an extension of who he is—a lovecat who shares knowledge, his network, and compassion.

In this book, he tells the story of his friend Mike, who was president of Pizza Hut. Every Friday during his lunch hour, Mike called his MVCs—Most Valuable Customers—to say "thank you for your business."

One Friday, Mike called a customer in a poor neighborhood in south Dallas who ordered more than a dozen large pizzas a month for a year. "From the bottom of my heart," he told her, "I want to thank you for your business." Then he asked the mother, "Tell me why you order our pizza. What's your story?"

The mother told Mike her story of being a divorced mother of five children, three to eleven in age, and of how she worked three jobs to support them. She didn't want her kids to see their mom accepting public assistance so she worked virtually nonstop. She let the eldest order pizza as a kind of reward because "my kids really love pizza."

Mike was so moved by her story that he said, "Ma'am, I want to thank you for something entirely different than being a good customer. I want to thank you for being a good mother."

Who will this mother buy pizza from for the rest of her life? How many of her friends will she tell this story of the day the president of Pizza Hut thanked her for being a good mother? How many pizzas will they buy?

Will Mike tell that story with a misty eye to his team with whom he conceives a work positive lifestyle to remind them of how much they can believe in Pizza Hut as they achieve positive results?

Mike called to give and gained again.

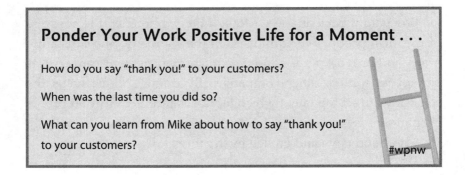

Ponder Your Work Positive Life for a Moment . . .

How do you say "thank you!" to your customers?

When was the last time you did so?

What can you learn from Mike about how to say "thank you!" to your customers?

#wpnw

Saying "thank you" to your customers because you receive a work positive lifestyle deepens your relationship with them so that everyone positively receives.

Do You Say "Thank You" to Your Employees?

A dear friend with whom I am also privileged to be a business partner is the general manager of a rapidly growing manufacturing company. One day over lunch, we discussed how we say "thank you" to employees rather than just assuming that we exchange money for their time and ability.

We talked about time off for family experiences like ball games and a grandbaby's birth. We mentioned flowers on Valentine's Day and other gifts on holidays.

Then we turned to the gift of presence that responds in more than the obvious, expected events of life. He told the story of how an employee was on the brink of financial disaster due to unforeseen life events. She had come to the operations manager about the situation and explained she may not be at her best productivity because of the stress. The ops manager shared the predicament with my friend who asked, "How much does she need?"

The OM said something about her inability to pay it back, but my friend simply said again, "How much does she need?"

The OM stated the amount, and my friend said, "Give it to her and tell her to pay it back as she can."

She paid it back as she could, a little at a time, and is now one of the most productive employees in the company. She constantly brags on her workplace and how much management cares for its employees, unlike other companies. By doing so, she helps the company attract top talent which increases productivity and profits even more.

My friend gave and gained even more.

Sure, not every company can lend money to its employees. In this case, it was appropriate.

A listening ear and a big shoulder to lean on cost you very little. Invest your ears and shoulders in your employees as your way of saying thank you.

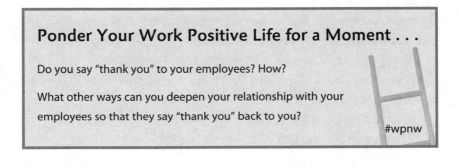

Ponder Your Work Positive Life for a Moment . . .

Do you say "thank you" to your employees? How?

What other ways can you deepen your relationship with your employees so that they say "thank you" back to you?

#wpnw

This Book Is My Thanks to You

As I am writing this book, I am tempted to think about how many copies it will sell. That translates into how much money I will make from those sales. That equates to a new home or beach house or lake house or sports car or . . .

Now of course I am perceiving, conceiving, believing, and achieving this book as a work positive result in my life. But what is my true underlying motivation that is revealed all too honestly as my reality redefines and my dream of this book fulfills?

Givers Gain.®

What goes around, comes around.

You reap what you sow.

Ultimately, I receive my work positive lifestyle.

I am very careful about what I have sown into this book because I know givers gain and that what goes around in this book will come back to me.

My motive in writing this book has nothing to do with *The New York Times* bestseller list, or speaking tours or monetary rewards, or the stuff those rewards make possible. Sure, they are nice, but . . . my motive is purely for your benefit. I desire to coach you to redefine your reality so you can fulfill your business dreams and enjoy a work positive life.

I know that in order to transform this negative world, it is going to take all of us working together to create a rising tide of positivity that will resolve our challenges as human beings so we can embrace our mutual dream opportunities.

This book is my way of saying "thanks" to you.

It is about you and me and everyone else on this planet learning to work positive.

So what else can I say, but thank you?

Thank you for the gift of your buying this book.

Thank you for investing your mental, social, emotional, physical, and ethical energies in positive ways in your business because of this book.

And what else can you say for the work positive life you have begun to enjoy as you have experienced this book, but thank you?

Can you imagine how much better our world will be when more and more and more of us start to say thank you for our redefined realities and fulfilled business dreams?

Just simply say "thank you" for your work positive life as you receive it.

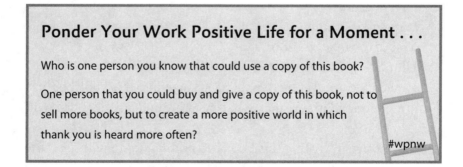

Ponder Your Work Positive Life for a Moment . . .

Who is one person you know that could use a copy of this book?

One person that you could buy and give a copy of this book, not to sell more books, but to create a more positive world in which thank you is heard more often?

#wpnw

Grab & Go

Remember these as you "Say Thank You."

1. Write a personal, handwritten "thank you" to someone at least once a week. Be specific with your gratitude.

2. "Givers gain.™" (Ivan Misner, BNI)

3. "What goes around, comes around."

4. "You reap what you sow."

5. Ultimately you receive your work positive life.

6. This book is about you. It is about you and me and everyone else on this planet enjoying a work positive business life.

7. Simply say "thank you" to your customers, clients, employees, vendors, and anyone else associated with your business as often as you can daily.

CHAPTER 19

Squeeze Yourself Dry

*"You cannot live a perfect day without doing something for
someone who will never be able to repay you."*

—John Wooden

If you put a sponge under running water, within a few minutes it
is saturated, correct? It can hold no more water.

But what if you left the sponge under the running water for
five more minutes? Would it hold any more?

Perhaps if you left the sponge under the running water for a
whole day it would hold more?

How about if you left it under the running water for a whole
week? Would it hold any more?

What would you have to do for the sponge to hold more water?

Squeeze it out, right? Only when you squeeze the sponge will
it hold more water.

As we enjoy a work positive lifestyle through our companies,
we are like a sponge. We can only soak up more of life when we
squeeze our lives and give away the positive we have received to
someone else. As we give away the positive results we received

in our businesses, then and only then do we create room within those same corporations for more of the beautiful, positive, reality-redefining, dream-fulfilling results.

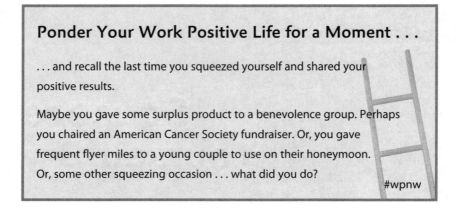

Ponder Your Work Positive Life for a Moment . . .

. . . and recall the last time you squeezed yourself and shared your positive results.

Maybe you gave some surplus product to a benevolence group. Perhaps you chaired an American Cancer Society fundraiser. Or, you gave frequent flyer miles to a young couple to use on their honeymoon. Or, some other squeezing occasion . . . what did you do?

#wpnw

Think about It This Way

If your hands are full, how can someone hand you something?

What if your hands are full, and someone wants to hand you something, and you want that something they are handing you more than what you are holding? What will you do?

Of course, you empty your hands to receive.

If we hang on to our most recent positive achievement so long that we begin to claim credit for it, our hands are full and we will not receive anything but the accolades and applause that accompany that experience. We deny ourselves the next great positive experience.

There is a penalty in college football for "bringing too much attention to oneself" after scoring. This rule intends to develop good sportsmanship among these young men in stark contrast to the NFL players they emulate who begin their bent-to-ego antics when in the act of scoring and continue them after the play to gain more celebrity status.

As in football, so it is as you work positive.

Ultimately, you work the important first four practices of perceive, conceive, believe, and achieve to the best of your ability, but it all comes down to the simple recognition that as your reality redefines and your business dreams are fulfilled, you receive your work positive lifestyle. Work positive is a team sport.

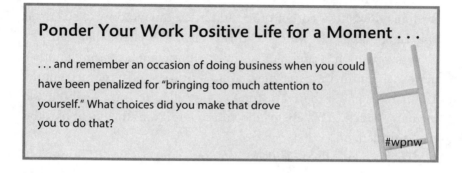

Ponder Your Work Positive Life for a Moment . . .

. . . and remember an occasion of doing business when you could have been penalized for "bringing too much attention to yourself." What choices did you make that drove you to do that?

#wpnw

Who Is Squeezing Whom?

A client requested a meeting with his banker one day and the conversation went something like this:

As you know, I have always paid on time when you have lent me money. I've always been very conscientious about making my payments and on time. However, currently I find myself in a bit of a jam. The people who owe me money are not paying at all instead of just a little late. I'm here today to request that you restructure my debt, extending the period longer, and giving me a grace period of 30 extra days to come up with a payment.

The banker agreed to the terms, had the contract drawn up, and both lender and borrower were satisfied.

As the client left the bank, relieved to have the new terms in hand, he saw someone walking on the other side of the street who owed him money.

"Hey!" he yelled loudly enough for everyone on Main Street to hear. "Come here, you. You owe me money!"

Running across the street while dodging traffic, he grabbed the guy's arm and said, "Where's my money? You think you can just take my money and not pay it back? That's a crime, my friend."

He forced the man into a nearby magistrate's office, filed a complaint, and had the man thrown into jail.

Meanwhile, the banker heard some commotion on Main Street from his third floor corner office and lifted the window to see what was happening. He watched in horror as the client that had just been forgiven his previous terms of payment accosted another man, drug him into the magistrate's office, and emerged alone. The banker knew the magistrate so he called to inquire about the incident. Much to his chagrin, he discovered that the client had the man imprisoned.

The banker then said to the magistrate, "Well, I have a complaint of my own to file." He rescinded the extension of terms for the client, and had the magistrate swear out a warrant for his arrest. Before the day was over, the client was in the jail cell next to the man he had imprisoned.

What goes around, comes around.

You reap what you sow.

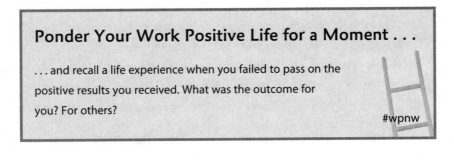

Ponder Your Work Positive Life for a Moment . . .

. . . and recall a life experience when you failed to pass on the positive results you received. What was the outcome for you? For others?

#wpnw

Remember the Daylilies and Birds

Like this client, you will be tempted to keep some positive results for yourself in fear that your business will run out. You choose the scarcity mentality—"There's not enough to go around!"—that we talked about in the second practice, "I Conceive," in the chapter about "Compare and Compete Rarely." The scarcity mindset believes, "I got mine and so you get yours" because there are a limited number of profitable slices of business pie.

Of course, this mental model is the antithesis of how the universe works with us. Remember the daylilies and the birds? They beautify and multiply quite prolifically with no concern for how much there is to go around, without limiting themselves by worrying. There is an abundance of resources that converge as we believe in our businesses and imagine the best these companies can be. The pie has infinite slices when we truly live into the work positive lifestyle. We will never run on empty.

I took my lawn mower to the shop for repairs. When I got it back to our farm, I cranked it up and started mowing. After a couple of passes, the engine started choking and coughing and finally just quit, and it wouldn't restart.

You can imagine what I was thinking: "This mower just came back from the shop and now it doesn't work. Where's the telephone?"

I called the repair shop, explained the mower's symptoms, and in as polite a voice as I could manage asked, "Now what's wrong with it?"

The kind, patient man with whom I was talking said, "Check the gas cap. There's a small screw valve on the top that we tighten down to keep the gas from spilling out when we turn the mower over. If we don't open it, the gas doesn't get any air. It's like it's running on empty."

When it seems like your business is running on empty, it is in that very moment that your focus has shifted from "Givers gain" to "Finders keepers, losers weepers." You are comparing and competing with others around the positive results you are receiving. Instead, open the valve to the doors of your business and let some positive air flow through you. Squeeze yourself dry immediately.

The universe in which you do business is wired to support you with abundance as you perceive, conceive, believe, and achieve positive results. Think about it like this:

Let's say I lend you a million dollars. At the end of one year, you agree to start making interest-free payments of $10,000 by the middle of each month until your loan is satisfied.

On the first of each month, I send you a check for $10,000 for you to use to make your monthly payment.

Get the picture now?

The greatest challenge you have in squeezing yourself dry is to trust that as you squeeze, you will receive more.

Get over yourself and trust the abundance of the universe, an infinite source of resources waiting to be yours as you work positive.

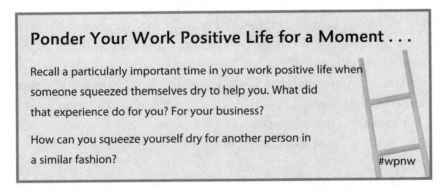

Ponder Your Work Positive Life for a Moment . . .

Recall a particularly important time in your work positive life when someone squeezed themselves dry to help you. What did that experience do for you? For your business?

How can you squeeze yourself dry for another person in a similar fashion?

#wpnw

Anticipate the Unexpected

One thing to anticipate as you squeeze yourself and your business dry is you will receive unexpected reactions. Some of them may be cut from the cloth of "Compare and Compete." Clemson University's former football coach, Frank Howard, told the story of driving in Greenville, South Carolina, one day. He saw a bumper sticker on the car in front of him that read, "Honk if you love God."

Howard said, "I loved God, so I honked."

When he did, the woman in the car in front of him, the car with the bumper sticker on it, got out of her car fighting mad, shook her fist at Howard, and said, "You fool, you want me to smack you? Can't you see the light hasn't changed?"

Sometimes, you do what you think is the right thing in squeezing yourself and your company dry, but you get an unexpected reaction. Sometimes what you do is misinterpreted by someone else. The other person doesn't "get" what you're meaning as you try to pass on positivity and success.

You and me and everyone else in the world is misunderstood at one time or another as we give to others because we have received. It happens. So what do you do? Explain when you'll be heard, ask for forgiveness when necessary, and just keep honking and squeezing.

Since you receive your work positive lifestyle as a gift, squeeze yourself dry and give positivity to others, trusting and ensuring that there is plenty in the universe's system to go around. As you squeeze your business dry, you discover that the more you give away, the more you receive. At the end of every month, you find more and more money, time, and opportunities.

That's when you adopt a work positive lifestyle of serving others.

Grab & Go

As you "Squeeze Yourself Dry," be sure to remember:

1. Squeeze a sponge so it holds more water. Squeeze your business so it holds more positive profits.

2. Empty your hands to receive. Empty your business, also, and make room for more.

3. There is a penalty in college football for "bringing too much attention to oneself" after scoring. The same penalty applies to business. Share the glory when you score.

4. When you feel like you are running on empty, it's because your business focus shifted from "Givers gain" to "Finders keepers, losers weepers."

5. Remember the daylilies and the birds. Your business receives all you need and more when you perceive, conceive, believe, and achieve at work.

6. There are more slices in the pie chart of your business than you can eat in a lifetime.

7. Anticipate the unexpected. Honk anyway.

CHAPTER 20

Serve Others

*"We make a living by what we get, but
we make a life by what we give."*
—Winston Churchill

One spring I hung a bird feeder in an oak tree just outside one of my office windows. I really like watching cardinals and there are lots of them in my part of the world.

I looked them up on the internet and discovered the kind of bird feed they prefer—sunflower seeds—and put lots of them in the feeder. Since then, about a dozen different families of cardinals have come to my feeder. Of course, they're not all there at once, but they do all get to feed there.

The key, I have discovered, is offering them what they prefer. I wanted them to come and visit me so I gave them what they wanted.

That is pretty much the way the work positive lifestyle works. When you give, you receive. Think of it as a universal life principle that is woven into the fabric of our everyday lives at work and at home.

- Givers gain.
- What goes around comes around.
- You reap what you sow.

Have an Attitude of Gratitude

Another key I have discovered is to give and receive primarily because you are motivated by thanksgiving. Your business is now prospering like it did previously only in your dreams. You are redefining your reality daily and learning the vast riches—time, money, relationships—of what it means to work positive. So out of an attitude of gratitude, you serve others. You give thanks for what you received in your company by offering others what they prefer.

The ways in which you can serve others are both uniquely yours and universally ours. Your unique contribution to make to the world through your business using your passion, gifts, and personality is yours to offer in service to meet the needs of others. It's at the corner of your contribution and the world's needs that the work positive lifestyle does business.

For example, I was talking with a man who runs a dry cleaning business. I asked him, "What do you find most fulfilling about what you do?"

He told me the story about how a family's home burned. One of the only things salvaged was the little girl's teddy bear. Now this teddy bear was in pretty rough shape. He had soot and stains all over him. He was soaked from the fire hoses and did not smell very good. The little girl absolutely loved this teddy bear and it was all she had left after the fire.

This businessman took on the mission of cleaning up the teddy bear. He worked on the little bear's soot stains until they were gone. He cleaned up and sanitized the bear so that he smelled all better. The dry cleaner said, "That was one happy little girl when I was through."

He went on to say, "And that's why I love to do what I do. I get to make a difference."

This man serves others, meeting the needs of the world, by making his unique contribution out of his work positive lifestyle. He makes a work positive life, not just a living, in a negative world.

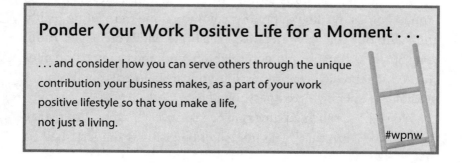

Ponder Your Work Positive Life for a Moment . . .

. . . and consider how you can serve others through the unique contribution your business makes, as a part of your work positive lifestyle so that you make a life, not just a living.

#wpnw

Small Acts of Huge Kindness

We all have a unique contribution to make to serve others out of gratitude for the work positive lifestyle we receive. Yet universally we all share some common pathways of service.

You have read story after story of random acts of kindness. The person at the drive-thru window who pays for the coffee of the person behind them, who then pays for the coffee of the next person, and so on for up to 27 customers. The same type of generosity occurs at traffic toll booths.

You have held the door of a retail store for a physically challenged person to wheel in. You have let someone over into your lane of traffic. You have arrived at a fast-food counter simultaneously with another parent and motioned the other parent ahead of you, remembering the challenges of eating out with an 18-month old.

There is so much positive goodness in the world, particularly as we realize that while we perceive, conceive, believe, and achieve a work positive lifestyle, more than anything else we receive it.

Therefore we serve others, knowing that givers gain, that what goes around comes around, that you reap what you sow, yet primarily motivated by an internal attitude of gratitude for how we receive a work positive life.

It is as we serve one another out of the abundance of our businesses that the negative world becomes more positive. Like a rising tide, all the ships around us are lifted up and together, as human beings, we live out of our common hope to redefine reality and fulfill our collective dreams. I celebrate with you as you fulfill your business dreams and you celebrate with me as my companies succeed. That which was impossible appears before us and becomes possible. We achieve greatness together.

We discover such greatness as we serve each other. We realize the positive truth that "The first shall be last and the last shall be first."

Selfishness brings suffering. Why? The universe refuses to support it.

Service brings sustenance. Why? The universe was created to support it—givers gain; what goes around, comes around; you reap what you sow.

We do not serve others in order to be served. Receiving such service is a natural byproduct of how the work positive life—how we perceive, conceive, believe, and achieve positive results—enlarges our perceptions, converges more resources for our conceiving, strengthens our beliefs, and creates more achievements.

Serve Customers and Employees with Gratitude and Kindness

In *Love is the Killer App*, Tim Sanders tells the story of Tom Ward, CEO of Barton Protective Services. Tom was brought in to lead the company in turning the ship around.

One of the first things Tom did was to go on the road and visit all the local sales offices. He particularly enjoyed talking with

Barton employees who were caught "doing something right." These women and men served their customers in a uniquely effective manner. Tom asked them to take a marker and draw him a map on a white board of how they did it. Tom honored the outstanding service of these employees by sharing their methods and giving them the credit. Barton then instituted these innovations in their customer relationships, offering the best service possible.

Such CEO-level service is rare, but evidently it pays huge dividends. Barton Protective Services was selected by Fortune as one of the Top 100 companies to work for, achieving that distinction four years running, and was the only security company ever selected. The company grew exponentially in revenue while lowering employee turnover and increasing customer retention. Tom Ward enjoys a work positive lifestyle because he serves others—customers and employees.

Together, serving one another, we become more work positive oriented than any one of us alone. The world transforms from a negative place to a positive paradise.

Or, to put it another way, husbands serve their wives by selling shotguns to purchase baby cribs. Wives serve their husbands by buying shotguns back. And friends serve husbands and wives by giving the shotguns back.

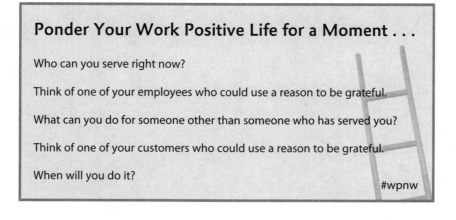

Ponder Your Work Positive Life for a Moment . . .

Who can you serve right now?

Think of one of your employees who could use a reason to be grateful.

What can you do for someone other than someone who has served you?

Think of one of your customers who could use a reason to be grateful.

When will you do it?

#wpnw

Grab & Go

"Serve Others" as you remind yourself:

1. Sell your shotgun to buy the crib. Watch as the shotgun returns.

2. Just like with birds, serve your customers and clients, employees and suppliers what they want, not what you think they should have.

3. Serve all your team members with an attitude of gratitude.

4. Love what you do for a living and use it to make a positive difference.

5. A rising tide lifts all ships . . . including yours.

6. The first shall be last and the last shall be first.

7. Together, serving one another, we make a work positive life, not just a living.

You Can Sustain Your Work Positive Lifestyle

"Few things in the world are more powerful than a positive push."
—Richard M. DeVos

C ongratulations! You have read this book.

Thank you for doing so. You see, most people buy books and never get this far, in fact, not much beyond the first few chapters. Your reading this far makes you more motivated than the rest to work positive.

These pages represent quite a journey for you.

You created some new neural pathways for perceiving your work positive life, discontent to dwell only in the Land of the Familiar ways you've done business. You chose to focus on and filter for the positive dimensions of your company even though you find yourself in a negative world.

You began to share those new perceptions with some other positive people, beginning complementary relationships of cooperation with them. You have kicked a few Eeyore Vampires to the curb.

You claimed your birthright to believe that there is another reality for your business, one in which you can believe and redefine your best as you begin to imagine what your company's best is. You give no emotional energy to your ego, choosing to bend toward the best while you watch resources converge that exceed your imagination.

All of your efforts to perceive, conceive, and believe that you can work positive emerge in results that you achieve. Your attention focuses on what is most important about your business, and, coupled with your intentions and actions for your work, you redefine your company's reality and fulfill your dreams of a work positive lifestyle. The impossible is now possible.

Now you discover that as an executive, entrepreneur, or business owner, you are grateful for the many influences and people that gave you the gift of a successful company. Your gratitude spills over from the heart of your business into the lives of others as you squeeze yourself dry daily and serve others through your business, taking advantage of opportunities that truly humble you. At the close of business, you know that you received your work positive lifestyle.

As my favorite brand of T-shirts says, "Life is good."

And yes, it will be. Your business life is eternally and perpetually rooted to work positive.

Here's a Word for the Journey

But let me offer you a word about the rest of your business journey:

It's not going to be easy.

I promised that you would become more positive in your work while doing business in this negative world.

And you have.

Continuing to grow as you work positive is the new challenge. That takes more than reading this book.

Remember the rubber band? How under no pressure, it lays there in your hand in one shape? But when you put it under pressure around that deck of cards, it takes on a whole new shape of more purpose?

You can continue to work positive once you put this book down, but it takes regular, consistent inspiration, instruction, and encouragement in this negative world.

Negativity will creep back in, like fog, on cat's paws, as you close the back cover of this book. Slowly at first. Almost imperceptibly. But count on it—the negative world definitely will try to wedge back into your business.

So what can you do to grow perpetually to enjoy your positive life? To receive regular, consistent inspiration, instruction, and encouragement?

You know how your doctor goes to classes to stay up to date on the latest techniques and treatments?

And how your CPA is required to do so many hours of continuing education to stay abreast of the latest tax law changes?

Your insurance agent must complete a certain number of units of education annually?

Why even massage therapists are regulated to participate in workshops to keep their skills sharp.

What if you could participate in similar groups of businesspeople with activities to aid you in growing to work positive more? What if you could:

- read a positive story weekdays just like the ones you read in this book so you can keep creating new neural pathways?
- subscribe to podcasts of these stories?
- participate in conferences and workshops with others who want to work positive like you?
- and enjoy some of those conferences and workshops at home in your pajamas—or in your office watching a video about

these five core practices, then discussing it with your team?

- have me lead your team meeting by phone?
- receive certification in the work positive lifestyle from an online university?
- and other, yet to be imagined, impossible-turned-possible ways of inspiring, instructing, and encouraging you in your pursuit of the work positive lifestyle?

Remember—my mission is more than to just write this book. My life mission is to coach so many businesspeople to redefine reality and fulfill their corporate dreams that the negative world is transformed into the positive paradise that it was intended to be from the start. My mission is to catalytically stimulate a rising tide of business positivity that lifts all the ships that desire to be lifted. My mission is to rediscover our positive commonalities as human beings who serve each other out of gratitude for the work positive lifestyles we receive.

By reading this book, you have joined this mission. I thank you.

And I invite you to continue the work positive journey.

There are already many, many of us. There is room for more.

All the resources you want in growing more positive in your work are available now. A few are developing that you and I have yet to imagine, but will want when we hear about them.

Let's work positive together.

Discover how simple it really is to sustain your work positive lifestyle daily. Go to www.ListentoLife.org or, call 1.877.4DRJOEY.

I wonder who will be the next Dale Carnegie, Colonel Sanders, Hewlett and Packard, Abraham Lincoln, Jerry Seinfeld, Michael Jordan, Thomas Edison, Alabama, John Grisham, Vincent Van Gogh, Tom Landry, Chuck Noll, Bill Walsh, Chuck Yeager, or _____ (insert your name here) because they chose to perceive, conceive, believe, achieve, and receive the work positive life?

Let's transform this negative world so we can all work positive.

Resources to Work Positive

Here are resources that I've found very useful in redefining my reality and making my business dreams come true in a work positive lifestyle. Most of them were recommended to me by the people I've interviewed and learned from over the years.

The resources are grouped to correspond with the five core practices for how you work positive in a negative world.

For an easy to use way to purchase these resources from Amazon, go to our website at www.ListentoLife.org.

Perceive the Positive at Work

James Allen: *As a Man Thinketh*
www.jamesallen.wwwhubs.com
The Great Depression produced so much positive perceiving literature. This one is a classic. Read it as soon as possible.

Gregory Berns: *Iconoclast*
www.ccnl.emory.edu/greg
Dr. Berns is a neuro-economist who teaches and researches now from Emory University in Atlanta. I learned a great deal from

him about how our brains process information—familiar and unfamiliar.

Dale Carnegie: *How to Win Friends and Influence People, Stop Worrying and Start Living*

www.dalecarnegie.com

As you read in the Introduction, Dale Carnegie wrote his first book during the Great Depression. Both of these books influenced me greatly during my youth. When in fifth grade, I entered an Optimist Club Oratorical contest on the recommendation of my English teacher. I was mentored by Toastmasters Club members. One of them suggested I read these books. I'm forever grateful I did.

Trainers around the world still teach Carnegie's philosophy and assist millions in transforming self-defeating behaviors through focusing and filtering their perceptions.

Malcolm Gladwell: *Blink*

www.gladwell.com

Gladwell is one of the best at integrating massive amounts of research into easy to understand themes that are transformational. *Blink* is a great example of how he helps us understand how we think.

Napoleon Hill: *Think and Grow Rich*

www.naphill.org

This is the platinum standard for focusing and filtering your perceptions for the positive. In fact, all five core competencies in some way find their roots in this classic. The Napoleon Hill Foundation preserves his influence and the University of Virginia campus at Wise, near Hill's birthplace at Pound, Virginia, continues some research and teaching of his principles. If you read only one of these resources, choose this one.

Maxwell Maltz and Dan Kennedy: *The New Psycho-Cybernetics*
www.psycho-cybernetics.com
Ever discover a book and wish you had found it years earlier?
Somehow I missed the original work but did find this Dan
Kennedy updated classic. Matt Furey directs a foundation
dedicated to continuing Maltz's legacy. Amazingly, Maltz was
a plastic surgeon who discovered more about how we process
internally than anything else in his practice. The impact of this
book on me is second only to *Think and Grow Rich* among the
classics.

Bob Nicoll: *Remember the Ice*
www.remembertheice.com
My friend Bob Nicoll walked into a convenient store one hot day
in Phoenix and with a simple suggestion of a semantic change
in a sign helped the owner immediately triple sales of ice. More
importantly, Bob discovered his own unique contribution to
make to the world—coaching us to focus on positive language
and filter out the "(k)notty" words.

Dr. Norman Vincent Peale: *The Power of Positive Thinking*
www.guideposts.org/norman-vincent-peale
If you've yet to read this book, stop what you're doing and order
it right now. Then read it. And re-read it. Dr. Peale continues
to improve positively generation after generation's thinking.
Focusing and filtering for the positive find their roots in this
classic.

Daniel Pink: *A Whole New Mind*
www.danpink.com
Dan Pink has influenced me through a series of books beginning with
Free Agent Nation which helped me start one of my businesses,
Listen to Life. This book introduced me to the Conceptual Age

in which we find ourselves now, having transitioned from the Information Age. The story-driven nature of *Work Positive* is because of Pink's findings. I even encouraged my older daughter to major in Creative Writing due to Pink's discoveries.

David Schwartz: *The Magic of Thinking Big*

www.cornerstone.wwwhubs.com/David_Schwartz.html

I discovered this book either at a yard sale or in the Goodwill store. Then, everywhere I looked, someone was referencing it. It's as much about "Believe" as it is "Perceive" but the title pushed me to include it here.

Conceive the Positive at Work

Keith Ferrazzi: *Never Eat Alone, Who's Got Your Back?, Relationship Masters Academy*

www.keithferrazzi.com

When I first read Keith Ferrazzi, my reaction was one of relief. Finally, I found permission to do what I am great at—relationships in business. Also, Keith is a master at systematizing relationship growth. Learn from him and you'll be an ultimate conceiver.

Malcolm Gladwell: *The Tipping Point*

www.gladwell.com

I've used this book in graduate classes I've taught ever since it came out. He takes your understanding of conceiving the positive to an upper level as he focuses your search on connectors, mavens, and salesmen. Whether you want to create a movement in your hometown or around the world, read this book and take aim at your tipping point.

Starr Hall: *Get Connected*

www.starrhall.com

Social media has made it possible for us to conceive with positive people around the planet 24/7/365. If you just aren't sure your business needs your "face" on a "book" or if you can learn how to tweet, get Starr Hall's book today. Read it tonight. Take action tomorrow and watch your business grow as you attract more of your ideal clients and customers.

Michael Port: *Book Yourself Solid*

www.BookYourselfSolid.com

Michael Port has done more than just about anyone to help me understand how to systematically attract more "ideal clients" into my business. Buy this book and be sure to download the guide from his website. Mine is in a three-ring binder on my shelf that I revisit on a regular basis. Michael is a generous soul and truly committed to conceiving the positive in all of our businesses.

Ivan Misner: *Masters of Networking*

www.bni.com

If ever there was anyone who understands the power of conceiving in what he calls "positive and supportive" ways, it's Ivan Misner. I've been a member of the company he founded, Business Network International, for years now. Every single year I have conceived with other positive people and found my referral network growing. Ivan helped refer me to my publisher and he and Beth are now friends of mine. Join a local chapter of BNI today to conceive a larger dream team of positive people than you ever imagined. No local chapter? E-mail Ivan and start one today.

Tim Sanders: *Love Is the Killer App, The Likeability Factor*

www.timsanders.com

I've used my friend Tim Sanders' books in graduate classes I've taught for years. The great thing about Tim's books is that as you sit down to read them, it's like having a conversation with a great friend that you want to spend even more time with. Tim makes my world a better, more positive place to live. He's an integral part of Team Joey.

Love Is the Killer App stimulated me to claim my inner "lovecat" by sharing knowledge, my network, and compassion through my businesses. *The Likeability Factor* prompted me to develop those parts of my personality that are pleasing to others and attracts them to do business with me. Both will help you do the same. Get both books today and enjoy your conversation with Tim.

Joe Vitale: *The Attractor Factor*

www.joevitale.com

This book helps you understand how we attract positive people and Eeyore Vampires. Joe was a major contributor along with Bob Proctor to *The Secret*.

Believe the Positive at Work

Claude M. Bristol: *The Magic of Believing*

www.claudebristol.wwwhubs.com

This book is yet another classic from another generation whose impact only strengthens with time. I am truly amazed by how timeless this book really is as it inspires this generation to believe in ways that defy imagination. To work positive, hypnotize yourself with the magic of believing.

Wayne Dyer: *You'll See It When You Believe It*

www.drwaynedyer.com

How do you choose from among so many great books by one author? I have no idea. So pick a book by Dr. Wayne Dyer. Any book with his name on the cover. And read it. Then get another one. And another one. And by the time you think you're caught up, he'll have written another one. Get that one, too and read it. You will be positively inspired to believe it until you see it.

Michael Gerber: *Awakening the Entrepreneur Within*

www.inthedreamingroom.ca

Michael Gerber is my hero. I have learned so much from his
   E-Myth books. I have coached "technicians having entrepreneurial
   seizures" using Gerber's techniques more hours than I can count.
   This book may be his best ever. Gerber's Dreaming Room is one of
   the most positive ways I've ever experienced to free more people
   to believe their unique contribution to the world can be made. If
   just one country on this planet would institute Gerber's Dreaming
   Room Awakening experiences as their economic development
   plan that country would positively zoom ahead of the rest of the
   world economy.

Dan Pink: *Drive*

www.danpink.com

Most of your business decisions are based on data, right? Like Joe
   Friday from *Dragnet*, you want "just the facts," correct? Dan Pink
   breaks new ground again by showing us what really motivates
   us to do business and our customers to do business with us. Dan
   just keeps lifting us higher and higher into understanding why
   we do what we do and how.

Michael Port: *The Think Big Manifesto*

www.thinkbigrevolution.com

Yes, I know "Think" is in Michael's title so you're wondering why
   it's under "Believe" instead of "Perceive." Michael Port pushes
   you to fill your work positive lifestyle tank with the jet fuel of
   your imagination. He truly believes that you can change your
   world, inspires you to do so, and shares with you how. Do
   yourself an immense favor and read this book. Watch as your
   business dreams grow and your reality redefines to make them
   come true.

Anthony Robbins: *Awaken the Giant Within*

www.tonyrobbins.com support@tonyrobbins.com

Whether I'm listening to one of his recordings, or reading one of
his books, or watching him on stage, I'm mesmerized by Tony
Robbins. He takes me deeper into myself so that I become a
true believer in the ultimate reality that all things are possible. I
particularly enjoy him on days I'm finding it difficult to believe
I can work positive. This was the book that launched it all with
him for me.

Patrick Snow: *Creating Your Own Destiny*

www.patricksnow.com

Patrick Snow is an incredible inspiration to so many. The "Dean of
Destiny" certainly believes at a level most of us aspire to. This
book sold so many copies as a self-published product that Wiley
picked it up. His systematic approach is easily duplicable for
your work positive lifestyle. Snow's frequent quotes raise the
motivation factor of reading exponentially.

Success **magazine**

www.successmagazine.com

Every time this magazine shows up in my mailbox, I devour it.
I even read the Letters to the Editor most of the time. Why? I
refuse to miss a single ounce of the inspiration ink dripping
from these pages. I especially enjoy popping the audio CD of
interviews that accompany each issue into my car's player. Want
to engage your emotions in creating a work positive lifestyle?
Subscribe today to this magazine.

Achieve the Positive at Work

Ken Blanchard: *The One-Minute Manager*

www.kenblanchard.com

Dr. Blanchard has influenced more of us to pay attention to
what's most important and act on it than perhaps any other

author. His Blanchard Companies training is legendary. This one book inspired a series too numerous to mention. Ken Blanchard knows how to achieve the positive at work. Read him. Practice him.

Stephen Covey: *The 7 Habits of Highly Effective People*
www.stephencovey.com
Every now and again there is a book written from the ages for generations to come. This one is destined to continue its positive influence on how we get things done at work and in our families. Covey knows how we best act on our attention and intentions. He is the master at helping us understand who we are, how we act best, and what success is truly about. If there is a rock star achievement author of our generation, Covey is it.

Entrepreneur magazine
www.entrepreneur.com
OK, they published this book. And I love Jere, Karen, Leanne, Jillian, and the rest of the dream team on the book publishing side. But I promise this is more than self-aggrandizement here. I have yet to remember when I first started reading this magazine. Yes, it was that long ago.

If you truly want to achieve a work positive lifestyle starting today, go to the website and get a magazine subscription. Read every word in every edition. You will discover the answer to every question you'll ever have about starting and running a business . . . including how to work positive in a negative world.

Tim Ferriss: *The Four-Hour Workweek*
www.fourhourworkweek.com
Tim Ferriss is the achievement guru for the New Rich generation. His global understanding of how to leverage attention and intention with an economy of action for the most return is excellent. I especially like the way Ferriss rivets your goals on

achieving more of that one non-renewable resource that we all want the most—time.

Dan Kennedy: *No BS Series*

www.dankennedy.com

I may have read every book Dan Kennedy has ever written, and some of them in different editions. His name may not be recognized as easily as some others here, but he really doesn't care. From books to coaching circles to infomercials, Dan's achievements are evidenced everywhere. His "No BS" series has one common theme: find a way to get done what needs doing and then move it out the door. Pick a book, any book with his name on it and read it. Today. Now. Why are you still reading this?

Brian Tracy: *The Psychology of Achievement*

www.briantracy.com

One of my partners and I were talking recently. We decided that Brian Tracy could very well be our generation's Napoleon Hill. Enough said? Go to a Brian Tracy International seminar—it will change your life. I suggest The Power of Personal Achievement Seminar, based on his Psychology of Achievement program.

Receive the Positive at Work

Bob Burg: *The Go-Giver*

www.burg.com

I love a great story. Bob Burg and John David Mann certainly know how to tell one. This book captures the essence of how we "receive" the work positive lifestyle—we put the other person first. That's why we "Say Thank You," "Squeeze Yourself Dry," and "Serve Others." This parable demonstrates how business functions at its best with all of us achieving success.

Leo Buscaglia: *Love*

www.buscaglia.com/about

Dr. Buscaglia left us too early but bequeathed us an inheritance that embodies the heart of what we "receive" in a work positive lifestyle. His University of Southern California course in "Love" always had a waiting list. This is a fun read that will transform how you say "Thank You" and "Squeeze Yourself Dry."

Robert K. Greenleaf: *Servant Leadership*

www.greenleaf.org

If you select only one book under this core practice, make it this one. The ten principles of servant leadership revolutionized how so many of us understand the way we best influence others to commit their hearts and minds to a common goal that's best for the most people. Treasure Greenleaf's work to truly "Serve Others."

James C. Hunter: *The Servant, The World's Most Powerful Leadership Principle*

www.jameshunter.com

Again, I love a great story. Jim Hunter knows how to write a great story and his heart is certainly in the "receive" place of "Serve Others" in *The Servant*. I love Jim Hunter's books. Read them and learn how to influence others in the most powerful manner known to humanity—as a servant.

Ivan Misner: *Networking Like a Pro*

www.businessnetworking.com

You already know I belong to a BNI chapter and am a huge Ivan Misner champion. Here's the major reason: Dr. Misner builds his success on a philosophy of "Givers gain.™" Go back and re-read that section of this book. It makes all of the difference in your business.

Bob Nicoll: *Exceptional Care*

www.remembertheice.com

So many of us talk about customer service as if it were an addendum to our business plan. My best friend in Alaska, Bob Nicoll, reminds us that how we take care of our customers determines how they share with us. You'll transform your vocabulary from "customer service" to "exceptional care" after reading this one.

Tim Sanders: *Today We Are Rich, Saving the World at Work*

www.timsanders.com

No one else has four books in this list. That tells you how highly I regard my friend Tim Sanders. *Today We Are Rich* is Tim's latest that takes his work in a direction to heights that are truly inspiring. In these two books, in addition to discovering why and how "receive" the positive works, you find the inspiration to do so. I especially enjoy the personal story of Tim's grandmother, Billye, and her influence on him.

Acknowledgments

My wife, Rowan, has believed in me since we were in college and became sweethearts. Your love completes me. You have my heart forever.

My daughters, Rebekah and Elizabeth, perceive me in ways I can only accept with gratitude. You girls will always have me wrapped around your little fingers.

My parents, Lonnie and Becky, conceived me and then remained faithful through the hard task of investing in me until today. Thanks for letting me grow up with you.

Leanne Harvey was the first one to take a chance on me. She perceived something special in this book . . . and in me. Thank you to her along with Jere Calmes, Jillian McTigue, Karen Billipp, and the rest of the incredible Work Positive Team at Entrepreneur Press. We all share alike in the positive transformations this book provokes. You are indeed the ultimate Work Positive Team, far better than I ever imagined.

Finally, thank you to my brother whom I chose, Michael Duncan, for looking me in the eyes daily for months on end, asking one question: "Where's my best seller?" Here it is, Michael. Enjoy!

Index

Dr. Joey Faucette sold inscribed Christmas cards door-to-door in the heat of summer as a 9 year-old when allergies prevented him from mowing lawns to buy a new bike. As a teenager, when told he'd have to pay for college, Dr. Joey discovered his excellent communication skills when, with no experience, he asked for and landed a job at a radio station where he launched what became the #1 rated afternoon show in that market. For 20 years, Dr. Joey led turn-arounds in small, medium, and large organizations, all of which set historical revenue and growth records.

A certified coach/consultant and member of the National Speakers Association, Dr. Joey has spoken professionally to thousands annually for nearly 30 years. He is a prolific writer of over 400 articles, has a syndicated radio show and newspaper column, and author of six books, the latest of which is *Work Positive in a Negative World* (Entrepreneur Press).

Since writing his first book ten years ago, Dr. Joey has appeared as a guest on hundreds of radio and TV shows across North America in most major markets. His website, www.ListentoLife.org, reaches people in 50 countries.

Corporations and organizations that invite Dr. Joey to speak discover these value-added returns on their investments:

- Achieve higher results through new solutions
- Increase productivity and lower employee turnover
- Coach teams to create collaborative relationships that broaden outcomes.

He and his wife have two adult daughters. They enjoy living on Pleasant Gap Farm with their five yellow Labs, three quarter horses, and one cat.

Invite Dr. Joey to Speak at Your Next Event

Whether you're a professional meeting planner or the chair of your association's event team, you will enjoy working with Dr. Joey Faucette and his team in planning your next experience. Much more than a "one-size-fits-all" presenter, Dr. Joey listens carefully to your needs, researches your industry, and surveys your audience before ever stepping on the platform. He brings the Work Positive message to your group in keynotes, workshops, and seminars.

Dr Joey Faucette's presentation really came at such a great time for our agents and their teams, especially for our customer facing team members. The "How to Work Positive in a Negative World" workshop coached and energized the agents and team members to positively achieve greater results by perceiving the positive mentally, conceiving it together as a team, believing in their customer relationships and products, and realizing they receive so much positive that can be reinvested in their businesses and communities.

> *"I enthusiastically recommend that you invite Dr. Joey to stimulate and coach your group to Work Positive!"*
>
> —MARINO RODRIGUEZ, INSURANCE EXECUTIVE, JACKSONVILLE, FLORIDA

To Book Dr. Joey for your meeting or event, contact
Arnett & Associates—Premier Speakers, Talent and Leadership

804.353.5999
www.arnettandassociates.com
Arnett & Associates Speakers
Arnett-Associates
@ArnettAssociates